RAILWAYS IN THE LAKE DIS⸺

Martin Bairstow

Introduction

It was the mineral wealth of Furness and West Cumbria which brought railways to this remote area in the late 1840s. The Furness Railway broke the isolation of the region by bridging the Kent and Leven estuaries and went on to develop the town and port of Barrow.

The railways were drawn deeper into the Lake District by the copper mines at Coniston, the ironworks at Haverthwaite, the quarries in Eskdale and by need to transport ore and coke across the breadth of the country.

Then came the early tourists for whom the railways catered with trains to the shores of the principal lakes, steamers on the waters themselves and primitive charabancs to reach the parts which the railway had never been able to penetrate.

When the real tourist invasion began in more recent times, the response was to close the lines which offered access to some of the most popular destinations, convert parts of their right of way into wider roads and turn some of the stations into car parks.

Meanwhile the freight for which the railways were built has all but disappeared leaving the sur-viving lines as virtually passenger only operations.

This book is about the lines which have served the Furness and Cumbrian Coasts as well as the Lake District itself. It is little more than an introduction. Maybe one day we could try for a second volume covering the subject in greater depth.

Thanks are due to Glynis Boocock for typing the manuscript from my scribble, to John Holroyd for help with artwork, to David Beeken for the excursion handbills and to Geoffrey Lewthwaite for the tickets. I am also indebted to Richard Pulleyn for the signal diagrams and to all the contributors of photographs which are credited individually. Thanks also to my wife Philippa for accompanying me on a number of car journeys to various destinations no longer accessible by rail, also to John Bateman who joined me on two similar ventures. If none of his photographs appear then that is testament to the appalling weather which we encountered.

Halifax, West Yorkshire
January 1995
Martin Bairstow

Familiar motive power on the Keswick line in BR days, Ivatt 2-6-0s Nos 46426 and 46458 pass through Troutbeck with an eastbound special on 13 June 1964. *(G.W. Morrison)*

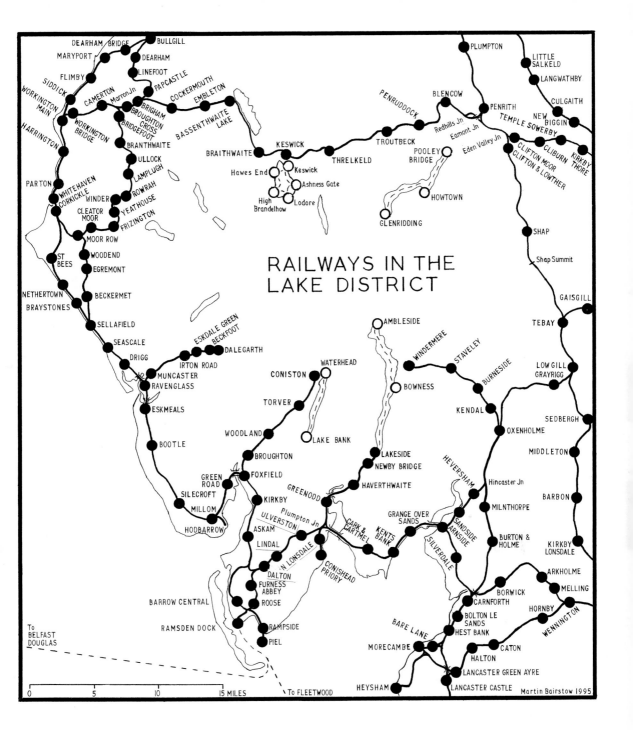

RAILWAYS IN THE LAKE DISTRICT

Martin Bairstow 1995

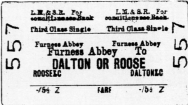

3

"With Running Water and Sanitation Nearby"

John F. Oxley recalls the end of an era

Class 50 NoD434 leaving Grange Over Sands with the 8.41am Barrow to Euston on 14 September 1968. Camping coaches in yard to the right. *(John F Oxley)*

The rhythmic throb of two Clayton diesels pounded across the still waters of Morecambe Bay on a warm, mellow, late summer evening. I moved to a window, lowered it by releasing the familiar railway leather strap and leaned out to enjoy the evening performance. Every weekday this westbound goods train (the term 'freight' had yet to become common parlance in the Sixties) well loaded with miscellaneous traffic for Barrow-in-Furness, came thumping by at a gait which spoke of the desire of the crew to get home just as soon as rules and signalmen would permit. It was 1968. Steam had just died on British Railways and some of the useless hulks still lay in Carnforth Shed just down the line but despite the mourning it had to be admitted that this performance by the conquering diesels had style.

It was also unarguable that I occupied a superb grandstand view of the old Furness Railway main line. My vantage point was provided by an erstwhile London & North Western Railway corridor coach, now doing duty with several others as a camping coach in the old goods yard at Grange-over-Sands. Despite being resplendent in a new coat of green and cream paint these and all the other camping coaches were soon to follow the steam locomotives (and the Claytons) into history. The Eastern Region

had disposed of their coaches abruptly some years ago, with the Southern and even the Western following suit soon after. Now only the Scottish and London Midland retained a diminishing fleet formed of the better vehicles mostly on coastal sites on the Furness, Cambrian and West Highland sections. Devotees enjoyed them while they could, but soon only the coaches at Dawlish Warren would survive, restricted to the use of British Railways Staff Association members.

What was the appeal of the camping coach? In their heyday they offered freedom to do as one liked, in contrast to the notorious régime of the boarding house, at a moderate cost particularly attractive to families. The requirement to purchase a given number of rail tickets was no problem when many people went on holiday by rail anyway. Holiday flats and static caravans were virtually unknown and only a well heeled minority had touring caravans. Camping in tents really needed a car, especially with children. So the camping coach had a virtual monopoly of a small but useful corner of the holiday market. They were quite spacious and handy for the station if one wanted to explore away from the chosen resort and many campers and the station staff became friends over a sequence of annual holidays. Even if the decor and fittings were a bit spartan it was recognised that they were after all camping coaches by definition and in those pre and early – post World War Two days the population at large lived happily enough without central heating, double glazing, indoor lavatories and the other essentials of life in the nineties. Anyway, as everyone knows, summers then were long and blissfully sunny and so spent outside. Finally, to railway enthusiasts and to the many others who took a lay interest in the passing train it was a wonderful opportunity to watch – and with co-operative railwaymen actually to participate in working – the traditional railway in its daily routine.

This idyll was destroyed by forces both without and within the railway. Rising standards of living made patrons less tolerant of the spartan life. Even the introduction of the Pullman camping coach with marginally improved amenities did little to stem the loss of business. The closure of branch lines and the (overdue) trimming of staffing levels eroded the availability of suitable sites and the staff to service them. Relaxing the rules on the purchase of rail tickets was exercised informally but, right to the end, the publicity specifically spelt out the requirement to buy rail tickets and many were deterred and lost at the earliest glimmer of interest. There was no such requirement in the case of the static caravans and holiday flats then spreading like wildfire through the holiday areas.

With the roar of the train fading into the golden distance I took a last look across the mudflats of Morecambe Bay and returned to the domesticities of camping coach life. The pots (if you are a Southerner read dishes – but Grange is in the North) and cooking utensils had already been washed and dried after the evening meal. No china and certainly no Teflon but plenty of elbow grease. No shortage of kitchen equipment generally but of a type that Mrs Beeton would have been comfortable with. Now to wash eighteen month old son before bedtime. Easy. Fill sink with hot water out of kettle, cool to taste and sit son in it while all concerned applaud the novelty. However, this taste of life without bath or shower was not so appreciated by the adults. Recourse to public baths – rarely available – had its drawbacks and to suggest bathing in the sea at Grange was a surefire way to acquire a reputation as a poor comedian. So most of the time it was a spongedown from a bowl carried into the bedroom or otherwise as discreetly as possible at the sink. For those who only took a bath once a week whether they needed it or not – and there were many in the Sixties – there was of course no real problem.

Lounging at ease in the standard camping coach was a relative term. Usually it meant perching on a hard wooden chair. Many found that a deckchair offered the greatest comfort and beach lilos were often pressed into service. No such problem in the Pullman coaches though – some of the deeply upholstered original seating was retained along with the fine panelling, brasswork and even the Pullman crests.

Four camping coaches at Grange Over Sands, 1968. The one on the left is at a platform obviating the need for a ladder. *(John F. Oxley)*

As the evening light faded recourse was made to gaslight (courtesy of Calor Gas) or to oil or Tilley lamps. Some found such illumination romantic and it certainly did wonders for the complexion, but others wished for the convenience of the electric light switch and quietly worried about the fire risk, gliding anxiously about the coach at "Lights Out" to ensure all lights were truly extinguished.

Bedtime was preceded by a trip down the yard to avail oneself of the station facilities, using the key provided to campers to avoid the need to put tuppence in the slot. Depending on the weather and the degree of baseness of the aforesaid facilities, this could be a chastening experience, although the women tended to have the better deal with their Ladies Room. The faint hearted resorted to the Elsan with which some coaches were equipped in an odd corner for emergency purposes, or to the more usual chamber pot. Beds were usually single or of the bunk type, wooden or metal framed; linen provided weekly by the railway.

Holiday activity and fresh air usually ensured a good night's sleep but if the coach was located close by an important line, as at Grange, the passage of trains during the night disturbed some campers. However they had usually got used to it by the time they had to go home! Even on quiet country branch lines, townies found the racket of nocturnal Nature equally disturbing and even alarming.

In the morning the cooking stove, usually Calor Gas driven, came into its own, boiling kettles and saucepans of water for morning tea and washing purposes, then producing delicious smells of frying fatty breakfasts as Mother reflects that her holiday consists of a change of cooking scene. 'New Men' had yet to be invented, although after breakfast the family might give a hand with the washing up, greasy pans being attacked with wire wool and the

Seascale looking south in April 1969. The camping coaches are still available for hire but the sidings have been disconnected and the signalling removed so the coaches will presumably have to be scrapped.
(Douglas Butterfield)

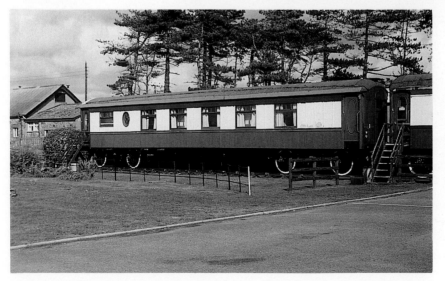

The two Pullman Camping Coaches are still at Ravenglass where they provide staff accommodation. They began life as first class Pullmans on the South Eastern & Chatham Railway in 1921. Second hand frames from LNWR ambulance trains were used in their construction. Named 'Elmira' and 'Maid of Kent', they were relegated to third class in 1948 as Nos 135 and 137 respectively becoming camping coaches in 1960.
(Martin Bairstow)

Mother discovers little respite from housework. Inside coach No. M021447M at Seascale September 1968.
(John F. Oxley)

bridget brush. Washing up liquid was still abhorred by many because it was said to make everything taste soapy!

If the weather was clement and a trip out was not planned, the deckchairs and folding stools and table would be heaved out of the storeroom and placed outside the coach. Visits to the station for various purposes usually involved chats with the staff in the booking office, the porters room or up in the signal box. The smaller the station the longer and friendlier were the chats. Quite often these would lead to reciprocal visits of staff to camping coach or by campers to railway cottage or on common ground in a local hostelry.

So the days would pass by, a round of idling by the coach and waving to passing trains, or down to the sea, or by train to some attraction not too far away, packed lunches and picnics, drinks at the local railway inn, perhaps even a meal out to give Mother a rest from cooking. The Swinging Sixties never quite penetrated the camping coaches, which remained firmly seated in pre-war Britain right to the end.

Sadly, it was not quite like that at Grange. Both in a railway and a tourist sense, the place was a bit too large and busy to fulfill the idyll. Furthermore, although it is indeed a lovely spot and many people return there year after year, it is not really suitable for lovers of the beach, young or old. The 'beach' of deep, gullied, sucking mud, is not only unpleasant but is also dangerous on a rising tide which floods so rapidly into Morecambe Bay that it produces something like the Severn Bore in its upper reaches. After an initial alarming experience followed by several days of beach deprivation clear signs of rebellion in the ranks could be seen, leading to an unusually long tour of the Lake District which just happened to call at a number of stations with camping coaches, including Seascale.

Seascale was different to Grange, not only in size. There were only two camping coaches, not in such good condition but adequate. They were parked well out of the way in the goods yard which was disused but still boasted a full complement of sidings and an array of red sandstone buildings, notably a tall circular derelict water tower, which induced something of an eerie feel to the place. The coaches looked not out to sea, which was obscured by the embankment carrying the coast line, but across to the distant Lakeland hills. But it had a super beach!

Enquiries revealed that both coaches were vacant for the following week, so immediately on our return to Grange I went to the booking office to request a transfer. The clerk was distantly polite, efficiently arranged the exchange but made it quite clear that he regarded it as a mortal insult to proud Grange-over-Sands that incredibly people could prefer Seascale! My wife could have told him but instead I mumbled my thanks and slunk back to the camping coach with the good news, received with acclamation.

So the very next day we packed up the car, paid for the Calor Gas, returned the precious toilet keys and decamped from the place in what might be described as an atmosphere. Quickly established at Seascale and welcomed by staff clearly delighted and relieved to have customers in their camping coaches, the family proceeded to enjoy a week of sun and bliss as they bathed in the remarkably warm waters of the Irish Sea, innocent of the hazards of the outfall from Sellafield and with no foresight of the future exploits of Greenpeace about that gently shelving, sandy beach.

Even so, signs of the approaching demise of the camping coach thrust upon our awareness when some condemned vehicles, including two Pullmans, paused for a day or two in the goods yard en route to their end in a bonfire somewhere or so I thought. I was glad to hear subsequently that the two Pullmans were in fact destined for the 'Ratty' at Ravenglass for use as sleeping accommodation, where they still repose.

Fate ordained that it was to be our last camping coach holiday, although we did not realise it when we left Seascale on a most filthy day as the weather broke. Other things distracted us and when the opportunity arose again it was too late, for they had all been withdrawn, an inevitable sacrifice to the new railway boasting of InterCity, Freightliners, MGR and so on and dedicated to the shedding of staff, country stations, superfluous lines and holiday trains. Camping coaches gave countless people wonderful holidays and made many friends for the railways as well as a useful income. Their demise was inevitable for social and economic reasons but to those of us who knew them and their diverse character they are sadly missed.

The title of this article is taken from a BR Publicity leaflet offering 'Spacious living-dining room with generous windows, well-furnished and skilfully planned. Compact, labour-saving kitchen, complete with china, glass and cutlery, and plenty of pots and pans'.

Not The West Coast Main Line

The Railway which we call the West Coast Main Line runs from London to Glasgow, a distance of 401½ miles. The alert traveller may actually see the coast momentarily as the train speeds past Hest Bank, just north of Lancaster. Otherwise the route is entirely inland. Clearly the name given to the line is to distinguish it from the East Coast Main Line rather than to imply any coastal connection.

Things would have been very different if George Stephenson, the 'Father of Railways' had had his way. In 1836 he was asked to report to the Whitehaven Committee of the Grand Caledonian Junction Railway on the relative merits of building the Lancaster to Carlisle Main Line via Shap Fell or via the Cumbrian Coast.

On 16 August 1837, Stephenson reported that he had made an 'Ocular Survey' of the rival routes and had found that the coast line would 'as nearly as he could measure from the map' be 22¼ miles longer.

Against this, he felt that 'if the line by Shap Fells be about 500 feet above the Coast Line, the merits of the two lines would be nearly equal in point of time in travelling between Lancaster and Carlisle'.

When he took into account 'the quantity of snow falling in high lands and the length of time it remains upon the ground and the effect produced by ice upon the rails retarding the engines', he concluded that 'a line across these hills would be interrupted by the severity of the winter for weeks together'.

So Stephenson's verdict came down in favour of building the Anglo – Scottish main line via the Cumbrian Coast. He expressed 'not the slightest doubt of the easy practicability of carrying the line across Morecambe Bay'.

His projected route was from Lancaster to Morecambe then by a causeway direct to Humphrey Head, south of Grange. The Leven would have been crossed more or less at the point of the present viaduct to reach Ulverston from where a tunnel would have pierced the higher ground in the Furness peninsula. Then another viaduct across the Duddon Estuary to Millom whence the Railway would follow the coast to reach Whitehaven from where a line was already authorised to Carlisle. At no point would the route have risen above 100 feet.

In 1839 the Government appointed two Commissioners to consider not just the relative merits of the alternative 'West Coast' routes north of Lancaster but also the rival claims that an Anglo –

Scottish main line might follow the East Coast route instead.

On the first question, the Commissioners found in favour of Shap rather than the Cumbrian Coast.

Had the decision gone the other way, and the coast route been built, then both the railway network and the landscape in general would have assumed a very different shape. The Shap route would doubtless have come later and taken on the main line function but the Furness District would have enjoyed more direct access and a lot of land would have been reclaimed in the process.

It was not to be. The Furness Railway did eventually bridge both the Kent and Leven estuaries, recovering quite a bit of land and offering a shorter route to Barrow than has ever been available by road. But the Morecambe Bay and Duddon Crossings remained elusive. The Cumbrian Coast has stayed a remote area requiring a circuitous journey whether by road or rail.

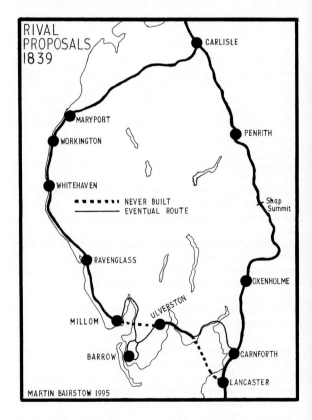

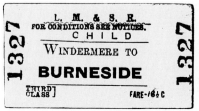

The Furness Railway

54252 and 53959 cross the Leven Estuary en route from Lancaster to Barrow whence they will continue right through to Carlisle, 11 October 1986. *(Tom Heavyside)*

The route which we now refer to as the Furness Line begins at Lancaster (we can hardly now describe Carnforth as the junction) and skirts Morecambe Bay to reach Barrow in Furness. The principal engineering features are the viaducts which carry the line over the Kent and Leven estuaries. The route is scenic with long stretches hugging the seashore.

At Grange Over Sands, the railway runs the length of the promenade. Here and at Ulverston the former Furness Railway stations are quite well preserved. Even at most of the smaller unstaffed stations, the buildings are retained albeit out of railway use. The line retains manual signalling with several of the original Furness boxes still in operation. Only at Grange has a 1950s BR flat roof box appeared in place of the authentic version.

For several miles, the railway marks the boundary of the cultivated land, some of which was reclaimed from Morecambe Bay during construction. On the seaward side the land is uncultivated. A few sheep manage to graze because it is only washed by sea water at very occasional high tides.

On fine days, there are views of the Lake District mountains to the north and across Morecambe Bay and towards the Fylde Peninsular in the other direction. Thanks to the two viaducts, the railway enjoys a considerable advantage in distance against

the road journey. In fact there are really only two blots on the landscape.

The first is Carnforth Station. This was the junction where the Furness Railway diverged from the West Coast Main Line. It once had an overall roof. In May 1970 BR closed and later demolished the main line platforms making it impossible to travel north from here or to Windermere or to connect from the Leeds or Barrow lines. Since 1990, the station has been unstaffed. Passengers enter through the old boarded up booking hall, then must walk along the fenced off up main line platform to reach the subway which leads them to the former Furness platforms where every doorway and window is also boarded up. The only relief from the dereliction is a small plaque on the wall recording that 'Brief Encounter' was filmed in a refreshment room here in 1949.

The other blot is a sign at the east end of Ulverston Station which proclaims 'Junction for Lakeside, Windermere and for Conishead Priory'. There is nothing unsightly about the sign itself so much as what it represents. It serves as a reminder that the destruction of just 4½ miles of railway has deprived us of rail access from the Furness Line right into the heart of the Lake District which is so choked with motor traffic.

Today the Furness line is virtually a passenger

A class 86 electric passes
through the demolished main
line platforms at Carnforth
with a northbound express on
19 May 1984.

(Martin Bairstow)

53966 leading the 9.22 Barrow-
Lancaster at Arnside on 20
September 1983.

(Tom Heavyside)

Crossing Arnside Viaduct
westbound in July 1958.

(Peter Sunderland)

only operation. The only surviving freight traffic is to and from the nuclear reprocessing plant at Sellafield on the Cumbrian Coast Line.

The original purpose of the Furness Railway was quite different. It was to convey minerals from the mines and quarries to the sea. It began as an isolated operation not connected to any other railway. Later it expanded, and took over other lines. It was directly responsible for developing the docks at Barrow and was the prime motivation in building the town there.

Beginnings

Prior to the Railway Age, the Furness District was very remote from the rest of the country because of the deep penetrations made by the Kent and Leven estuaries. The area was however rich in mineral deposits with iron ore mines near Lindal and Dalton and with slate quarries further north near Kirkby. Barrow was only a tiny village but it was sheltered by Walney Island and thus well placed to develop into a port.

The origins of the Furness Railway lay in the need for transport from the mines and quarries to the sea. Subsequent development was inseparably linked to that of the port and town of Barrow in Furness.

The principal landowners in Furness were the Duke of Buccleuch and the Earl of Burlington (later the Duke of Devonshire) who also owned the mineral rights. They provided a substantial part of the finance required to establish the railway.

The company was incorporated on 23 May 1844 with powers to build 14 miles of railway running from Lindal and Kirkby to the sea at Barrow and at Rampside. The terminus at Kirkby was to be connected by an inclined tramway to the Earl of Burlington's slate quarries which were located at an altitude of some 500 feet.

Earlier plans to continue beyond Lindal to Ulverston had been dropped for lack of any support from landowners in Ulverston. By early 1845, it had been decided not even to go as far as Lindal but for the time being to terminate at Crooklands, 1/2 mile east of Dalton, where a series of inclined tramways brought iron ore down from the mines.

The small network opened for goods traffic on 3 June 1846, a passenger service beginning during August. All lines were single track but the formation was built wide enough for double track which was laid during 1847 on the busiest section between Dalton and Roose.

During the first six years of operation, the company only had four locomotives. All were supplied by Bury, Curtis & Kennedy of Liverpool and were delivered to Barrow by sea from Fleetwood. No. 3, which ran until 1907, is preserved at the National Railway Museum in York.

The importance of the Rampside branch lay in the activities of John Abel Smith, a London banker who had built a causeway from Rampside out to Roa Island. There he planned to build a pier which would be accessible to ships at all states of the tide, unlike at Barrow. Smith had a financial interest in the Preston & Wyre Railway and it was his intention that ships should operate from Fleetwood to his pier at Piel on Roa Island.

The Furness Railway built an extension along Smith's causeway to Piel Pier. This opened in 1846 at the same time as the rest of the system. A ship, the 'Ayrshire Lassie' plied between Fleetwood and Piel affording a link with the embryonic national railway system.

Relations between the Railway company and Mr Smith appear to have been strained. The steamer service was diverted to Barrow for a time. During the winter of 1848-49, the Railway closed the Rampside/Piel branch.

In 1852, Smith joined forces with some local businessmen in seeking Parliamentary powers for an independent line from Piel to Lindal. The Furness Railway successfully opposed this then sought to buy Smith out. It was helped in this quest by a freak storm which reduced the value of Smith's property.

A 3 1/2 mile extension took the Furness Railway north from Kirkby to Broughton. Authorised in July 1846, this line aimed to draw traffic from the copper mines at Coniston. It opened in February 1848.

Extension to Ulverston

The initial indifference of Ulverston towards the railway soon evaporated. Even as the first trains began to move on the Furness Railway in June 1846, revised plans were being advanced to extend from Crooklands to Ulverston.

The line was authorised on 27 July 1846. Work began straight away but was stopped in June 1848 as the Furness Railway felt the effects of the post 'Railway Mania' depression.

Work resumed the following year but only as far as Lindal to which point a single line was opened on 6 May 1851. The route was extended a further mile to Lindal East on 27 May 1852 but Ulverston was not reached until 7 June 1854.

Temporary station buildings were erected at Ulverston but these blew down in a gale on New Year's Day 1855. They were replaced by a permanent station but this was soon relegated to become the goods depot when the line extended eastwards.

The Ulverston & Lancaster Railway

The isolation of the Furness Railway was brought to an end in 1857 with the completion of the very difficult 19 1/2 mile link between Ulverston and Carnforth, where connection was made with the Lancaster & Carlisle Railway.

This line was built by an independent company, the Ulverston & Lancaster Railway. This enjoyed the support of the Furness and was able to call on loans from the Dukes of Buccleuch and Devonshire during construction.

Prominent amongst the promoters of the Ulverston & Lancaster were the Brogden family who had developed iron ore mines at Stainton, near Ulverston. In 1850 they purchased the Ulverston Canal which allowed their ore to reach the sea for onward transport to ironworks in Staffordshire.

Authorised in July 1851, and opened on 1 September 1857 the Ulverston & Lancaster Railway began at a junction with the Furness Railway just west of Ulverston. It was not possible to project the line eastwards from the Furness station because it was at too high a level. For a short time trains reversed out of the terminal in order to reach the new route until through platforms could be provided at the present Ulverston station.

Dominant features between Ulverston and Carnforth are the viaducts over the Leven and Kent estuaries. With respective lengths of about 600 and 500 yards, these began as single line structures each with an opening span in order to preserve navigation to the ports of Greenodd and Milnthorpe.

They were widened to double track during the 1860s when the opening spans were abolished. Greenodd was bought off with the promise of a branch line. Milnthorpe had to resort to litigation which resulted in a small jetty being built at Arnside.

The original cast iron girders were replaced by wrought iron on both viaducts during the mid 1880s. Then, during the First World War, brick piers were built around the cast iron columns. This work altered the appearance of the structures considerably.

Stations in Barrow

The original 1846 station was a wooden structure with a single platform. It was located close to the later Buccleuch Junction but on an alignment slightly to the north. It was converted into an engine shed after the second station opened on 29 April 1863.

In January 1871, the tracks leading into the original station were removed when the main line was diverted as part of the work of building Buccleuch Dock.

The 1863 station was at Barrow Strand near the north west corner of Buccleuch Dock. It was enlarged in 1873 when the former carriage shed was converted into an arrival platform. The name Barrow Town was adopted in 1881 but by this time, its days as a passenger station were almost over.

Congestion in the dock area made it desirable to divert passenger traffic on to an entirely new route which would form a 5¼ mile loop from Salthouse Junction, through a new Barrow Central Station then continuing close to the Duddon Estuary to meet the Whitehaven line at what is now Park South Junction (originally Thwaite Flat Junction).

The Barrow Central scheme was authorised in 1872 but work did not commence straight away and it was not completed until 1 June 1882. Barrow Town then became a goods depot.

0-6-0 No. 12511, built for the Furness Railway in 1920, is seen at the east end of Barrow Central Station in 1931. The loco only lasted one more year.   *(G. Coltas)*

Barrow Central had a large overall timber roof spanning platforms 1 and 2 which were linked by a subway. Platform 3, the outer face of the island, stood outside the overall roof but was protected from the elements by a projecting awning. An additional bare platform 4 was added in 1906, largely for the benefit of excursion traffic.

Much of the station was destroyed during an air raid in May 1941. The platforms were then exposed to the elements until 1958 when new buildings were provided in contemporary BR style with steel frames and multi-coloured rustic bricks.

A station opened at Island Road on 1 May 1899 to cater for shipyard workers who arrived on trains from Grange and from Millom which were not advertised in the public timetable. Initially there was only one platform but a second one was added in 1915.

Trains approached over the Buccleuch Bridge and were withdrawn at the end of 1966 after this had been declared unsafe.

Ramsden Dock station was built in 1885 though temporary facilities had been available there since transfer of the Belfast and Isle of Man boats four years earlier. It was used by trains connecting with these and later the Fleetwood sailings but closed in 1915 after the First World War brought an end to regular passenger shipping from Barrow.

The other surviving station at Barrow in Furness is Roose. This opened about 1850 just north of the junction between the two original branches of the Furness Railway: to Barrow and to Piel. Roose is now an unstaffed halt with only the most basic platform shelters by way of facilities.

Barrow Docks

'Some day Barrow will become a Liverpool' – so claimed W. E. Gladstone, then Leader of the Opposition, at the opening of Devonshire Dock on 19 September 1867.

The Furness Railway provided Barrow with four docks. Devonshire and Buccleuch were created by enclosing the area between the town and Barrow Island. Occupying about 31 acres each, they were opened in 1867 and 1873.

The 67 acre Ramsden Dock was authorised in 1872 and opened on 24 March 1879. It was connected to Buccleuch Dock through a breach in the embankment which carried the railway onto Barrow Island. At first an 80 foot span swing bridge was provided. This was replaced on 12 October 1907 by a lifting bridge upon which the two railway tracks were interlaced so as to leave room for road vehicles.

Not satisfied, the Furness Railway also sunk a fortune into the 146 acre Cavendish Dock. Barrow had the third largest docks in England after London and Liverpool but it did not have the volume of shipping to justify the investment. Cavendish Dock was never fully used.

In 1864-66 and again in 1871 and 1872, the Furness Railway paid a dividend of 10%. That was when the iron and steel traffic was at its peak. They managed to pay 7% in 1882 but only 1/2% in 1895. The average for 25 years 1887-1911 was less than 2 1/4%. The company never achieved the hoped for return from the docks.

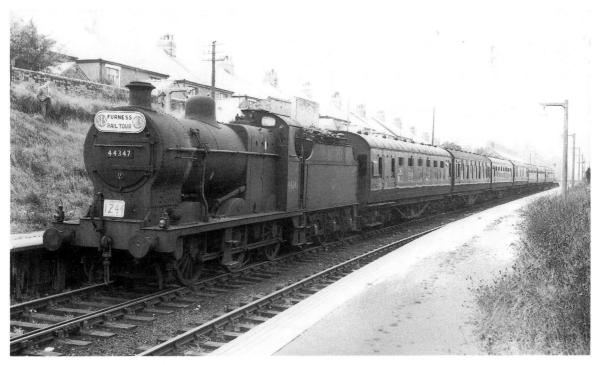

4F 0-6-0 No. 44347 at Island Road Station on 27 August 1961.   (John Marshall)

156460 leaves Barrow in Furness with the 10.48 to Manchester Airport on 9 July 1994. This is the same station as that illustrated on page 12.
(Martin Bairstow)

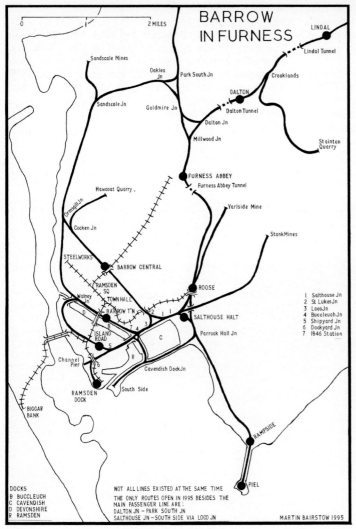

BARROW IN FURNESS

0 — 2 MILES

LINDAL
Lindal Tunnel
Sandscale Mines
Oaklea Jn
Park South Jn
Crooklands
DALTON
Sandscale Jn
Goldmire Jn
Dalton Tunnel
Dalton Jn
Millwood Jn
Stainton Quarry
FURNESS ABBEY
Furness Abbey Tunnel
Hawcoat Quarry
Yarlside Mine
Ormsgill Jn
Cocken Jn
StankMines
STEELWORKS
BARROW CENTRAL
RAMSDEN SQ
Walney Jn
TOWN HALL
BARROW T'N
ROOSE
SALTHOUSE HALT
ISLAND ROAD
Parrock Hall Jn
Channel Pier
Cavendish Dock Jn
RAMSDEN DOCK
South Side
BIGGAR BANK
RAMPSIDE
PIEL

1 Salthouse Jn
2 St Lukes Jn
3 Loco Jn
4 Buccleuch Jn
5 Shipyard Jn
6 Dockyard Jn
7 1846 Station

DOCKS
B BUCCLEUCH
C CAVENDISH
D DEVONSHIRE
R RAMSDEN

NOT ALL LINES EXISTED AT THE SAME TIME
THE ONLY ROUTES OPEN IN 1995 BESIDES THE
MAIN PASSENGER LINE ARE:
DALTON JN – PARK SOUTH JN
SALTHOUSE JN – SOUTH SIDE VIA LOCO JN

MARTIN BAIRSTOW 1995

James Ramsden was appointed locomotive superintendent of the Furness Railway in 1846 at the age of 23. He became secretary and manager four years later and directed the affairs of both the Railway and the town of Barrow until his death in 1896. He now dominates Ramsden Square. *(Stuart Baker)*

The Piel Branch

As already mentioned, this branch was part of the original Furness Railway of 1846.

Piel gained in importance with the transfer of the Midland Railway Belfast service from Morecambe in 1867 but lost this trade in favour of Ramsden Dock in 1881.

As a result of this, direct access onto the Piel branch from Roose was removed in 1882 but a local service continued from Barrow to Piel using a curve built in 1873 between Salthouse and Parrock Hall Junctions. The 1910 timetable shows four trains each way Mondays to Fridays with six on Saturdays but none on Sundays. This remained the standard of service until the branch closed in 1936. An additional halt was opened at Salthouse on 22 May 1920. It had one short wooden platform with no facilities apart from a tiny hut serving as a booking office. It did not feature in the public timetable.

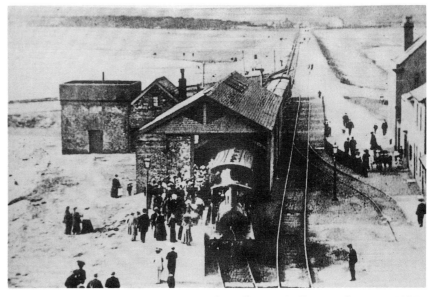

Furness Railway 2-4-0 No 75 has arrived at Piel with a good load of day trippers from Barrow. The train has crossed the causeway from the mainland built by John Abel Smith. *(Stuart Baker collection)*

Departures from Barrow Central April 1910

To Carnforth	To Whitehaven	To Piel
7.05am	5.23am	8.05am
MO 7.35	8.25	SO 11.15
8.45	11.10	SX 12.35
9.45	SO 12.30pm Kirkby	SO 1.25pm
12.25pm	SO 1.40 Silecroft	5.55
1.05	2.50	8.25
1.50	4.58	SO 10.10
3.40	5.45 Millom	
4.13	7.35 Millom	No Sunday service
5.40	8.15	
7.40	9.40 Askam	
9.00	SO 11.00 Millom	**To Ramsden Dock**
SO 11.00 Ulverston		Tuesdays, Thursdays
		and Saturdays
Sundays	Sundays	8.18pm
7.10am	5.23am	
10.30 Lakeside	9.15	
4.45pm	6.50pm	
7.40		

MO = Mondays only SO = Saturdays only
SX = Saturdays excepted

Departures from Barrow in Furness Summer 1994

To Lancaster		To Carlisle	
1.55am	Preston	6.12am	Carlisle
6.33	Manchester Airport	6.55	Carlisle
7.20	Liverpool Lime St	SX 8.35	MIllom
7.45	Manchester Airport	SO 8.43	Millom
8.41	Manchester Airport	10.00	Millom
9.20	Lancaster	SX 10.22	Carlisle
10.48	Manchester Airport	SO 10.30	Carlisle
11.06	Lancaster	11.42	Carlisle
12.16pm	Lancaster	1.38pm	Millom
12.43	Manchester Airport	2.57	Carlisle
1.34	Lancaster	3.40	Sellafield
2.46	Manchester Airport	5.11	Carlisle
3.31	Lancaster	5.53	Millom
4.25	Lancaster	7.09	Millom
4.48	Manchester Airport	9.00	Millom
5.40	Preston		
7.10	Preston	No Sunday service	
SO 9.30	Preston		
SX 9.48	Preston		
Sundays			
8.50am	Manchester Airport		
10.20	Manchester Airport		
12.25pm	Manchester Airport		
2.05	Manchester Airport		
3.10	Manchester Airport		
3.45	Lancaster		
5.28	Manchester Airport		
8.30	Manchester Airport		

31275 approaching Grange with nuclear flasks for Sellafield on 17 October 1987. *(Tom Heavyside)*

Grange Over Sands is well restored but now staffed for only part of the day. *(Martin Bairstow)*

'Black Five' 4-6-0 No 45293 passing Kents Bank 'wrong line' due to engineering work on Sunday 13 February 1955.					*(J.C.W. Halliday)*

47427 approaching Plumpton Junction with the 10.09 Preston to Barrow on 28 July 1982.

(Tom Heavyside)

L M S
LONDON MIDLAND AND SCOTTISH RAILWAY.

M 3451

BANK HOLIDAY, AUGUST 3rd, 1931,
SPECIAL EXCURSIONS
to
Ulverston, Greenodd, Haverthwaite
Lake Side, Bowness & Ambleside

From	Departure Times		RETURN FARES—THIRD CLASS—TO					
			Ulverston	Greenodd	Haverthwaite	Lake Side	Bowness	Ambleside
	a.m.	a.m.	s. d.	s. d.	s. d.	s. d.	s. d.	s. d.
Barrow	8 30	9 50	1 0	1 6	2 0	2 0	3 6	4 0
Roose	8 34	9 54	1 0	1 6	1 6	2 0	3 6	4 0
Furness Abbey	8 39	9 59	0 10	1 3	1 6	2 0	3 6	4 0
Dalton	8 44	10 4	0 6	1 1	1 5	1 6	3 0	3 6
Lindal	8 49	10 9	0 5	0 11	1 3	1 6	3 0	3 6
Ulverston	9 10	10 25	...	0 6	0 10	1 3	2 9	3 3
Greenodd	9 18	10 33	...	...	0 5	0 9	2 3	2 9
Haverthwaite ...arr.	9 25	10 40	...	...	...	0 5	1 11	2 5
Lake Side ...arr.	9 35	10 50	...	...	...	...	...	...
Bowness	10 20	11 55	...	...	...	...	...	...
		p.m.						
Ambleside	10 55	12 30	...	...	...	...	...	...

Passengers return same day by **any ordinary boat or train** or following special :—

							p.m.
Ambleside	...	...	...	...	...	...	7 10
Bowness	...	...	...	...	...	...	7 40
Lake Side	...	...	...	...	...	...	8 35
Haverthwaite	...	...	...	...	...	...	8 40
Greenodd	...	...	...	...	...	...	8 50
Ulverston	...	...	...	...	...	...	9 5

Children under 3 years of age free ; 3 and under 14 half-fare.

LUGGAGE ALLOWANCE.
Passengers holding day or half-day Excursion Tickets are not allowed to take any luggage except small handbags, luncheon baskets or other small articles intended for the passengers' use during the day. On the return journey only, passengers may take with them free of charge, at owner's risk, goods for their own use not exceeding 60 lbs.

Tickets, Bills, and all particulars can be obtained in advance at the Stations, or from the following :— **Barrow**—Messrs. THOS. COOK & SON, LTD., 61, Duke Street.

Conditions of Issue of Excursion
and other Reduced Fare Tickets.
Excursion Tickets, and Tickets issued at Fares less than the Ordinary Fares, are issued subject to the Notices and Conditions shewn in the Company's current Time Tables.

Further information may be obtained on application to the Divisional Passenger Commercial Superintendent, Hunt's Bank, Manchester.

July, 1931.   (CXM.2712/A)   **J. H. FOLLOWS, Vice-President.**

The clock tower dominates the 1874 station at Ulverston.
(Stuart Baker)

Ulverston has platform faces for only two tracks, a feature which used to assist passengers changing for Lakeside. The 1.45pm Lancaster to Barrow calls on 11 October 1986. *(Tom Heavyside)*

Train Services on the Furness Line

The accompanying tables show the standard of passenger service available from Barrow in 1910, when the Furness Railway was in charge, and in the current timetable for 1994/5.

The 1910 table shows the basic year round service and does not include summer extras or excursion trains. Nor does 'Bradshaw' make clear the range of through carriages leaving Barrow for destinations on the LNW and Midland Railways.

The LMS timetable for May and June 1934 is rather more specific. This shows a 7.10am from Barrow conveying through carriages to both Manchester Victoria and Leeds Wellington. The 9.12am departure includes through carriages from Cockermouth and Workington to London Euston. The 1.10pm from Barrow is through both from Whitehaven to Euston and from Barrow to Leeds and the 5.30pm has a through carriage from Whitehaven to Bradford Forster Square.

Through trains from Barrow to London ceased in 1977 although there are plenty of opportunities to make the journey with a change at Lancaster or Preston in less time overall than would have been taken in the days when through carriages were shunted around at Carnforth.

The May 1994 timetable saw the introduction of through trains to Manchester Airport. Generally these run hourly from Lancaster starting back at either Barrow or Windermere. They run via Preston, Wigan, Bolton, Manchester Oxford Road and Piccadilly. On the Furness Line these trains mostly stop only at Ulverston, Grange and Carnforth leaving some of the small stations with a service fractionally worse than previously.

Overall the standard of passenger service today is at least as good as in any previous timetable. By contrast freight has declined to the point where virtually the only traffic passing along the Furness Line is that destined to or from the nuclear reprocessing plant at Sellafield.

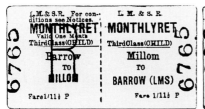 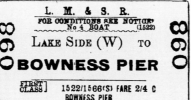 

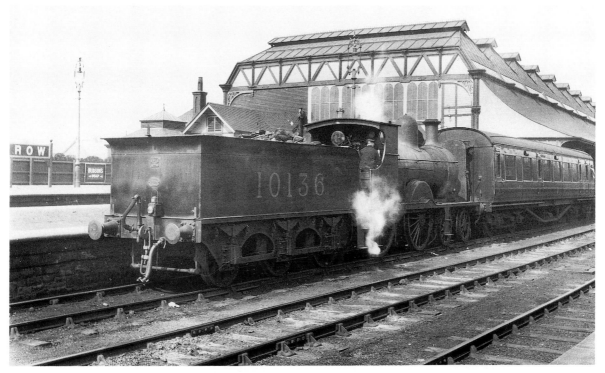

No. 10136, ex Furness Railway No. 37, a 4-4-0 dating from 1896 stands in platform 3 at Barrow Central in 1931, the year in which it was withdrawn. *(G. Coltas)*

Dalton Station has lost its canopy and its staff since this view was taken towards Barrow in 1969.
(Douglas Butterfield)

A Barrow bound 'Derby Lightweight' set about to enter Furness Abbey Tunnel (76 yards) on 11 April, 1966.
(John Marshall)

Furness Railway 0-4-0 No. 13 at Barrow on 12 August 1902. The loco dating from 1858 was then at the end of its life and had acquired the No. 13A to make way for a new No. 13 which had been delivered in 1899.
(LCGB Ken Nunn Collection)

The Conishead Priory Branch

Authorised in 1876 and opened on 27 June 1883, the short branch from Plumpton Junction to Conishead Priory was built as double track as it was hoped that it might eventually be extended round the coast to Barrow. This would have avoided the gradients on the existing route with the need to bank freight trains in both directions up to Lindal.

An intermediate station opened at North Lonsdale Crossing in June 1888 but the branch never lived up to expectations. For many years there was only one passenger train each way leaving Ulverston at 11.55am and returning from Conishead Priory after a six minute turn round at 12.13pm.

In common with a number of lightly used branch lines, Conishead Priory closed to passengers on the last day of 1916. The branch was abandoned beyond North Lonsdale but was retained to that point in order to serve first the ironworks which closed in 1938 then the Glaxo chemical works which ceased using rail transport only very recently. Now (in 1994) the truncated branch is disused.

On 27 August 1961, 3F 0-6-0 No. 43282 ventured as far as North Lonsdale with the Furness Railtour.

(D.J. Mitchell)

Conishead Priory Station in 1966, almost 50 years after closure.

(John Marshall)

Arnside to Hincaster Junction

Furness industrialists were amongst the promoters and financiers of the South Durham & Lancashire Union Railway. Incorporated in 1857 and opened in July 1861, this line ran from Barnard Castle in County Durham to Tebay on the West Coast Main Line passing over Stainmore Summit. Absorbed by the Stockton & Darlington Railway at the beginning of 1863, it became part of the North Eastern later that year.

The initial Furness interest in the Stainmore route was as an outlet for haematite to ironworks in the North East. In the event, the main traffic flow was the other way with coke being brought from South Durham to feed the new blastfurnaces near Barrow.

In 1865, a 5¼ mile 'cut off' was authorised to give direct access on to the Furness Line at Arnside from the West Coast Main Line at Hincaster Junction, south of Oxenholme.

Progress in building the line was slow. A contract was let in 1871 but it did not open until 26 June 1876. Neighbouring landowner George Wilson of Dallam Tower had sufficient influence to force the line to cross the River Beela on 'arches and pillars'. The result was a 26 arch viaduct running parallel to the Kent Estuary with cast iron spans over the river itself approached by stone arches on either side. The ornate station of Sandside with its chalet style overhanging roof was also a sop to Wilson.

From sea level at Sandside, the line climbed 200 feet in two miles, an average of nearly 1 in 50. This proved a deterrent to heavy freight traffic and the coke trains continued to run via Carnforth until the First World War when congestion there compelled the use of adequate motive power to go via Sandside.

A passenger service was operated by the Furness Railway between Grange Over Sands and Kendal. For many years this operated five times per day weekdays only. 'Bradshaw' for July 1938 shows an enhanced service of seven trains with two on Sundays. There are also one or two unusual trains booked over the branch on Saturdays including one through from Northampton to Barrow via Oxenholme.

In pre grouping days, the Midland Railway operated through carriages from Leeds to Windermere. These were detached from a Barrow train at Arnside then worked on via Sandside. Another unusual passenger service over the branch was that provided by the North Eastern for the benefit of Durham miners visiting the convalescent home at Conishead Priory.

The local passenger service ended in May 1942. The line closed north of Sandside in September 1963 but was kept open to serve the quarry there until January 1972.

Sandside looking towards Arnside

(Stuart Baker Collection)

The Cumbrian Coast Line

A Carlisle to Barrow dmu has just left the remote station of Nethertown on 6 September 1985.

(Tom Heavyside)

Built to tap the mineral wealth of this rather isolated region, the Cumbrian Coast Line has outlived almost all the traditional industries whose fortunes it used to share.

If there is a single reason for the route's survival, it is the nuclear reprocessing plant at Sellafield. Not only does this give rise to the transport of spent nuclear fuel in steel flasks but it also generates some commuter traffic from places along the coast which have lost most of their traditional employment.

As a tourist route, the Cumbrian Coast Line has much to commend it. All the way from Barrow to Maryport, the sea is never far away. From Seascale to St Bees, the line runs along a ledge on the cliff directly overlooking the sea. On a clear day you can just make out the Isle of Man from here. Then north of Whitehaven the line twists with the seashore, a very slow stretch of line part of which, just beyond Parton, has had to be reduced to single track in order to make room for better defences against avalanches.

Connection is made at Ravenglass with the narrow gauge line into Eskdale. Another attraction is the Visitor Centre at the Sellerdale Plant but tourist potential is hampered by the great disadvantage of this route, its remoteness from any major centre of population. A journey from the south requires a detour into Barrow usually with a change of train there. Then there is the long sweep round the Duddon Estuary in order to reach Millom, 25¼ miles by rail from Ulverston but only seven as the proverbial crow would fly.

The entire route from Barrow to Carlisle was completed in November 1850. It was built by a number of independent companies who were not brought under unified management until the 'grouping' in 1923. We have already seen that the Furness Railway penetrated as far north as Broughton in February 1848. By that time a line was being projected southwards along the coast to meet it.

The Maryport & Carlisle Railway

This enterprise, the northernmost link in the chain, falls outside the scope of this book. Suffice it to say that it was an early line incorporated in 1837 and opened in stages between 1840 and 1845. It remained an independent company until it was merged into the LMS in 1923.

The Whitehaven Junction Railway

With Maryport rail connected, Whitehaven feared a loss in importance. The principal landowner there was Lord Lowther (later the Earl of Lonsdale) who commissioned a report from George Stephenson on the practicality of a railway along the coast.

The result was the incorporation in July 1844 of the Whitehaven Junction Railway. Construction proceeded quickly. The first section from Maryport to Workington opened on 19 January 1846 and was at first worked by Maryport & Carlisle rolling stock. Operation was extended to Harrington on 18 May 1846. The line reached Whitehaven for goods on 15 February and for passengers on 19 March 1847.

Serving the most heavily industrialised part of the coast, the Whitehaven Junction resisted efforts by the Maryport & Carlisle to persuade it to amalgamate with its northern neighbour. Instead, in 1865, it was taken over by the London & North Western Railway with which it had become connected upon completion of the route between Penrith and Workington.

The Whitehaven & Furness Junction Railway

This, the next link southwards in the coastal chain, was incorporated on 21 July 1845. The principal backer was again the Earl of Lonsdale who seems to have been persuaded by George Stephenson that extending the railway further down the coast offered the best chance for realising the area's mineral wealth. The original plan involved a 1¼ mile viaduct across the Duddon estuary to join the Furness south of Kirkby.

The 'Railway Mania' was now at its height. Before any work had been done on its already authorised route, the Whitehaven & Furness Junction went on to promote a Bill for a Lancashire Extension. Largely anticipating what was to happen during the following decade, this proposal would have involved a line from Dalton to Carnforth crossing both the Leven and Kent estuaries. Furness tracks would have been used from near Kirkby to Dalton, presumably with a direct curve. The Bill failed to make any progress in Parliament.

As the 'Railway Mania' gave way to recession, the Furness & Whitehaven Junction was forced to rethink plans for its coast line. By an Act of August 1848, the Duddon crossing was abandoned in favour of a route going round the estuary with a shorter viaduct across the River Duddon near Foxfield. Connection was made with the Furness Railway one mile south of Broughton with the junction facing Broughton rather than Barrow.

Work had already begun at the Whitehaven end. The first section opened as far south as Ravenglass on 21 July 1849. Bootle was reached on 8 July 1850 and Broughton on 1 November the same year. The initial timetable offered three trains on weekdays and two on Sundays from Whitehaven to Broughton with connections to Barrow. The 10.30am from Whitehaven, first and second class only, offered onward connections via Piel and Fleetwood to Preston and beyond. The single line was virtually flat, the main engineering features being the five timber viaducts over the Rivers Calder, Irt, Mite, Esk and Duddon. The last named was a 592 yard timber trestle with 50 spans.

Traffic from Whitehaven to Barrow had to reverse at Broughton until 1 August 1858 when the junction was turned the other way. A new station was provided at Foxfield at the joint expense of the W & F J and the Furness Railways. Broughton was left at the end of a short branch line but a year later, the original terminus closed in favour of a through station with the extension of the line to Coniston.

The W & F J was taken over by the Furness Railway in 1865. Encouraged by the discovery of haematite at Hodbarrow near Millom, the W & F J obtained fresh powers for a line across the Duddon estuary. Not content with joining the FR on the other side, it proceeded in 1865 to obtain powers to go on

Coal Board 0-4-0 ST No. 8 shunts on Whitehaven Harbour near the foot of the rope worked incline from Haigh Colliery on 14 May 1971.
(Tom Heavyside)

A 0-4-0 crane tank dating from 1890 still in service at the haematite mine at Hodbarrow on 19 March 1967. After closure of the mine and the Hodbarrow branch on 31 March 1968, the loco was acquired for preservation at the Lytham Motive Power Museum. *(John Holroyd)*

to Lindal thus bypassing part of the FR mileage. The Furness responded by taking over the W & F but on terms which reflected the latter's new found prosperity in haematite traffic.

The new owners set about improving the coast line. By 1874, the track had been doubled as far north as Sellafield and all the wooden viaducts replaced by cast iron structures. However, the Furness Railway failed in what should have been the greatest innovation.

A contract had been let in 1867 for construction of the Duddon Viaduct between Millom and Askam. Materials had already been brought to site when the Furness Railway decided to call off the project which was abandoned officially by an Act of August 1869.

Parliament was well used to being asked to abandon railway lines which it had previously been prevailed upon to authorise, not least in the period of the late 1860s when the trade cycle had moved again into recession. It ventilated its frustration with the Furness Railway by legislating that mileage rates for fares and freight charges should be calculated as if the direct route had been built and not via Foxfield.

The clause was particularly penal on traffic coming out of the mines at Hodbarrow to which a 1¾ mile branch from Millom had been opened in 1867. This branch should have been the first stretch of the direct line across the Duddon.

Whitehaven Tunnel
The terminus of the Whitehaven Junction Railway was at Bransty on the site of the present station. When the Whitehaven & Furness Junction Railway opened southwards, it started from a station at Newtown, later known as Preston Street. At first the only physical connection between the two systems was via the Harbour branch which passed through the street.

A direct link had already been authorised under the W & F J Act of 1846 but the only way to get through the town was by means of a 1,333 yard tunnel which proved very difficult to bore because it penetrated a number of old mine shafts.

The tunnel opened on 30 September 1852 but passenger trains did not run through to Bransty from the south until 3 December 1855. Newtown then became the main goods depot for Whitehaven. A replacement passenger station opened at Corkickle, close to the south portal of the tunnel. Bransty still remained a terminal station, trains from the south having to reverse at William Pit then set back into the platforms. It was not until 24 December 1874 that through platforms were provided adjacent to the north portal of Whitehaven Tunnel.

The single line tunnel was lined with red sandstone and brick. By the 1920s it had become distorted in places and was constantly undergoing repair. Piecemeal work failed to remedy the situation and in 1932 the task began of relining it throughout, a job which was to take 26 years. Because of the limited clearances, work in the tunnel required a complete possession for five or six hours every night. Clearances were improved marginally and the tunnel was shortened by 33 yards at the south end.

Train Services Along The Coast
A list of departures from Barrow to Whitehaven is given on page 15 for 1910 when the Furness Railway was at its zenith and for 1994 when who knows whether British Railways may have been at its peak.

On both occasions there are six through trains shown which nowadays all go through to Carlisle. The journey has become faster over the intervening 84 years. In 1910 it took between 1 hour 27 and 1 hour 55 minutes for the 45¾ miles. Today's diesel units do it in 1 hour 9 to 1 hour 20 minutes. All the intermediate stations are still open apart from Eskmeals but since 1977 trains have called by request at the less important ones. Only Askam, Millom, Ravenglass and Sellafield remain compulsory stops.

The short workings to Millom cater for the denser volume of traffic between that town and Barrow whilst the afternoon Sellafield working brings workers back from the nuclear plant when it returns at 4.40pm.

The most dramatic change is that today's passenger trains are in a majority on what used to be primarily a freight route. One of the last flows of traffic to be lost was oil from Whitehaven to Purfleet which disappeared during 1994 leaving the goods terminal at Preston Street, near Corkickle, disused.

All that remains is traffic to and from Sellafield including nuclear waste imported via Ramsden Dock which still retains a rail connection from Salthouse Junction on to the south side of the dock.

Park South box, viewed to the north, controls the junction between the Dalton loop and the route, now single track, out of Barrow. The sidings north of the crossing have been removed since this photo was taken in 1969.
(Douglas Butterfield)

A Barrow to Carlisle dmu has just left Seascale on 6 September 1985.
(Tom Heavyside)

Green Road looking towards
Foxfield in 1969.
(Douglas Butterfield)

Millom looking towards
Whitehaven in 1969 since
when the platform canopy has
been transferred to the narrow
gauge station at Ravenglass.
(Douglas Butterfield)

Silecroft looking north, also in
1969.

(Douglas Butterfield)

4F 0-6-0 No. 44449 travelling north through Ravenglass with a mineral train on 6 July 1957.

(J.C.W. Halliday)

Two preserved 'Black Five' 4-6-0s Nos 45407 and 44871 approach Ravenglass with empty stock from Sellafield which is going to work a return special from Ravenglass to Carnforth on 5 May 1973.

(Tom Heavyside)

Nethertown, looking north in April 1969 with BR style signal box still controlling the passing loop, since removed.
(Douglas Butterfield)

The 10.35am Barrow to Carlisle emerges from Whitehaven Tunnel and calls at Bransty Station on 21 July 1979.

(Tom Heavyside)

0-6-0ST 'Warspite' approaching Harrington Coal Preparation Plant with a load from the BR exchange sidings in May 1971.

(Tom Heavyside)

Ex Midland Class 2P 4-4-0 No. 40695 prepares to depart Whitehaven Bransty with the 1.22pm to Carlisle on 13 April 1953. *(John F Oxley)*

The 1.05pm Whitehaven to Carlisle dmu hugs the coast just south of Parton on 21 July 1979. *(Tom Heavyside)*

Former Southern Railway 4-6-0 No. 850 'Lord Nelson' negotiates the curve through Parton with the 'Cumbrian Coast Express' on 28 July 1982. *(Tom Heavyside)*

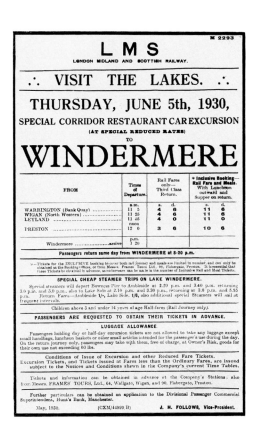

M 2293

L M S
LONDON MIDLAND AND SCOTTISH RAILWAY.

∴ VISIT THE LAKES. ∴

THURSDAY, JUNE 5th, 1930,

SPECIAL CORRIDOR RESTAURANT CAR EXCURSION

(AT SPECIAL REDUCED RATES)
TO

WINDERMERE

FROM	Times of Departure.	Rail Fares only— Third Class Return.		* Inclusive Booking— Rail Fare and Meals. With Luncheon outward and Supper on return.	
	a.m.	s.	d.	s.	d.
WARRINGTON (Bank Quay)	11 5	4	6	11	6
WIGAN (North Western)	11 25	4	6	11	6
LEYLAND	11 45	4	0	11	0
	noon				
PRESTON	12 0	3	6	10	6
	p.m.				
Windermere ....arrive	1 20				

Passengers return same day from WINDERMERE at 8-20 p.m.

∗—Tickets for the INCLUSIVE booking to cover both rail fares and meals are limited in number, and can only be obtained at the Booking Offices, or from Messrs. Frames Tours Ltd., 91, Fishergate, Preston. It is essential that these Tickets be obtained in advance, as no increase can be made in the number of Inclusive Rail and Meal Tickets.

SPECIAL CHEAP STEAMER TRIPS ON LAKE WINDERMERE.

Special steamers will depart Bowness Pier to Ambleside at 2.20 p.m. and 3.40 p.m. returning 3.0 p.m. and 5.0 p.m., also to Lake Side at 2.10 p.m. and 3.30 p.m., returning at 3.0 p.m. and 5.55 p.m. Return Fares—Ambleside 1/-, Lake Side, 1/6, also additional special Steamers will sail at frequent intervals.

Children above 3 and under 14 years of age Half-fares (Rail Journey only).

PASSENGERS ARE REQUESTED TO OBTAIN THEIR TICKETS IN ADVANCE.

LUGGAGE ALLOWANCE

Passengers holding day or half-day excursion tickets are not allowed to take any luggage except small handbags, luncheon baskets or other small articles intended for the passenger's use during the day. On the return journey only, passengers may take with them, free of charge, at Owner's Risk, goods for their own use not exceeding 60 lbs.

Conditions of Issue of Excursion and other Reduced Fare Tickets.
Excursion Tickets, and Tickets issued at Fares less than the Ordinary Fares, are issued subject to the Notices and Conditions shewn in the Company's current Time Tables.

Tickets and information can be obtained in advance at the Company's Stations; also from Messrs. FRAMES TOURS, Ltd., 64, Wallgate, Wigan, and 90, Fishergate, Preston.

Further particulars can be obtained on application to the Divisional Passenger Commercial Superintendent, Hunt's Bank, Manchester.

May, 1930.   (CXM/44999 B)   **J. H. FOLLOWS, Vice-President.**

L M S
LONDON MIDLAND AND SCOTTISH RAILWAY.

Weekly Holiday Contract Tickets
FOR "RUN-ABOUT" HOLIDAYS.

Commencing on May 1 until October 31, 1932

Weekly Holiday Contract Tickets will be issued, available for an unlimited number of journeys by any Ordinary Train between the following points :—

LANCASHIRE COAST and .
LAKE DISTRICT RESORTS.

BETWEEN

CONISTON, BARROW, FURNESS ABBEY,
WINDERMERE (Lakeside), WINDERMERE (L & N W),
MORECAMBE, LANCASTER, PRESTON,
BLACKPOOL, FLEETWOOD and SOUTHPORT,

ALSO BETWEEN

AMBLESIDE, BOWNESS and LAKE SIDE

ON WINDERMERE STEAMERS

(Does not include conveyance between Windermere (L & N W) and Bowness).

First Class 15/- Third Class 10/-

The Holiday Contract Tickets will also be available by any Special Day or Half-Day Excursion Trains advertised between any Stations within the area covered by the Tickets during the period of their availability.

Tickets can be obtained on application at any Station within the areas mentioned above.

Half-rate Tickets issued to children under 14 years of age.

They are England's best travel value to-day !

E 594A
(E.R.O. 53207)   **C. R. BYROM, Chief General Superintendent.**

The Whitehaven, Cleator & Egremont Railway

What may appear at first sight to have been a heavily engineered duplicate route running parallel to the Coast Line, was in fact built to exploit the rich seam of iron ore, about a mile wide, which extended south from Lamplugh towards Egremont.

From the early 1840s, this mineral wealth was developed by the Whitehaven Iron & Steel Company who built an iron works at Cleator Moor. Progress was, however, impeded by dependence on primitive road transport to and from the coast.

To overcome this defect, the Whitehaven, Cleator & Egremont Railway was incorporated in 1854 and opened for goods on 11 January 1856. Commencing at Mirehouse Junction, a mile south of Corkickle, it climbed steeply for two miles to Moor Row. Here a branch turned northwards passing Cleator Moor before reaching a terminus at Frizington. The main line continued southwards to Egremont.

A passenger service began on 1 July 1857 starting from Corkickle rather than Bransty in the absence of any agreement over the cost of running powers through Whitehaven Tunnel. The Frizington branch was extended to Rowrah on 1 February 1864 and further to Marron Junction on the Cockermouth & Workington Railway on 2 April 1866. The entire system was built as a single track but was progressively doubled over a period lasting until 1874 when activity in the iron industry was approaching its peak.

Traffic from Egremont heading towards Barrow had to be conveyed via Mirehouse Junction, a situation which the W, C & E sought to remedy by promoting a 5 mile extension southwards to Sellafield. Faced with losing this traffic over its own mileage between Mirehouse and Sellafield, the Whitehaven & Furness Junction opposed the Cleator Company's proposal preferring to build the Egremont to Sellafield link itself. Compromise ensued and on 28 June 1866, the two companies were empowered to build the link jointly. It opened on 2 August 1869 by which time the Furness Railway had taken over the Whitehaven & Furness Junction interest.

In 1877, the W C & E agreed to be taken over by the London & North Western Railway but the Furness objected successfully and was able to force a joint takeover. From 17 June 1878 therefore, the W C & E became the North Western & Furness Joint Line. In general the LNWR operated the passenger service and freight north of Rowrah, the Furness operating freight south of this point.

'Bradshaw' for April 1910 shows six departures from Whitehaven to Rowrah, some going on to Workington via Lamplugh and Camerton. There are five services to Sellafield via Egremont, some requiring a change at Moor Row off the Rowrah train. There is an additional lunchtime working to Beckermet and an evening one to Egremont but no Sunday passenger trains on any part of the W C & E.

Passenger services were withdrawn in April 1931 between Moor Row and Marron Junction and in January 1935 from Corkickle to Sellafield via Moor Row and Egremont. The latter service was reintroduced briefly in 1946/47 and there were some unadvertised workmen's trains between Moor Row and Sellafield until September 1965.

The former W C & E lines closed to goods traffic in stages between 1954 and 1980.

Former Furness Railway 0-6-0 No. 52494, built 1913, leaving Rowrah with a pick up goods for Workington on 13 April 1953.

(John F Oxley)

Woodend looking towards
Moor Row in April 1969.
(Douglas Butterfield)

Beckermet looking north also
in April 1969.
(Douglas Butterfield)

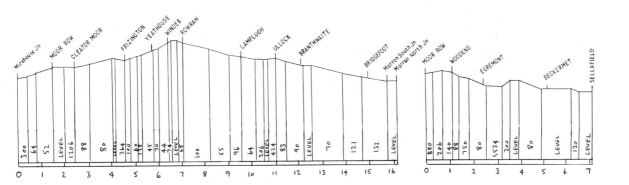

The Kendal & Windermere Railway

51799 leads a Metro Cammell set up the final climb into Oxenholme with the 10.30am from Windermere on 6 May 1989. *(Tom Heavyside)*

The one surviving branch line in the Lake District runs for ten miles from its junction with the West Coast Main Line at Oxenholme to the town of Windermere.

Since 1973 it has been 'a pointless railway' a term used by the contemporary national press, not to suggest that the line had become futile, but to condemn the removal of all the points. Not only was the line singled, it was reduced to just a long siding extending from the bay platform at Oxenholme to the buffer stop at Windermere. Only one dmu is allowed on the branch at a time. Loco hauled trains cannot be accommodated at all.

In the 1970s, the Windermere branch was rather lucky to escape the same fate as Keswick. More recently its fortunes have been restored. Since May 1994 it has even enjoyed a through service to Manchester Airport.

The Kendal & Windermere Railway was promoted when it became apparent that the West Coast Main Line was going to miss Kendal. According to Joseph Locke, engineer to the Lancaster & Carlisle Railway, the problem lay not in getting into Kendal so much as getting out again. A Kendal Railway Provisional Committee instructed their own surveyor to challenge Locke. The rival scheme involved a 2¼ mile tunnel north of Kendal so perhaps Joseph Locke's theory had been proved.

Accepting that they had lost this argument, the Kendal committee redirected their efforts into promoting a branch line which would run from Oxenholme through Kendal to Windermere.

The line was authorised in June 1845. Work was concentrated on the first two miles in order that Kendal could become rail served upon the opening of the southern portion of the Lancaster & Carlisle Railway on 22 September 1846. It then took only until April 1847 for the double track branch to be completed through to Windermere.

Though nominally independent, the Kendal & Windermere borrowed most of its locos and rolling stock from the Lancaster & Carlisle by whom it was leased in perpetuity (effectively taken over) in 1858. The following year, the Lancaster & Carlisle was itself leased by the London & North Western Railway placing the entire West Coast Main Line from London to Carlisle under one management.

More of the early history of the Windermere branch will appear in *The Preston, Lancaster & Carlisle Railway* by Peter E. Baughan which we hope to publish fairly soon.

One of the promoters of the line, Cornelius Nicholson foresaw the advent of long distance commuting when he prophesied that the day might come when trains from Manchester to Windermere would 'bring the merchant and manufacturer after he has finished his correspondence or left the Exchange, down to the shore of that beautiful lake and if he likes carry him back next morning in time for breakfast'.

The accompanying list of departures for April 1910 shows the up 'Windermere Express' leaving at 8.30am Mondays only. The corresponding down working was at 5.07pm from Manchester Exchange on a Friday arriving Windermere at 7.12.

By 1922 the Express was running daily Mondays to Fridays with a through carriage from Liverpool Exchange joining the train from Manchester at Preston. The LNWR provided a club car for the benefit of first class season ticket holders with all the facilities of a gentlemen's club including a subscription and a committee.

The club car disappeared with the outbreak of the Second World War but the train itself ran until 1966 after which Windermere was quickly reduced to a local service only, a state of affairs which was to last until 1994.

Returning to the 1910 timetable, this represents the all year round service then on offer and is clearly more comprehensive from Kendal than from Windermere itself. If we move forward to the Summer timetable for 1938, then we find Windermere with some 20 departures Mondays to Fridays, slightly more on Saturdays but only four on Sundays.

These are only the timetabled passenger trains. In those days, there would have been at least an equivalent number of other train movements with freight, parcels, light engines, excursions etc. It is when this factor is taken into account, that today's 'slim line' railway becomes a much quieter affair than its predecessor.

The Windermere branch retained some steam working right to the last weekend of regular steam operation on BR. The last steam loco on the branch left Kendal goods yard, light engine plus brake van on Saturday 3 August 1968.

Windermere closed to goods in April 1969, the coal merchants being forced to retreat to Kendal. Then in May 1972 Kendal yard suffered the same fate, this time the coal merchants being given the choice of collecting from Lancaster or having their deliveries brought all the way from the collieries by road.

The only remaining goods on the branch was to Cropper's private siding at Burneside but that finished later in 1972. About the same time, Kendal's parcels traffic ended following a switch to road transport by the biggest customer, K Shoes.

When the branch was singled in 1973, no facility was left at Windermere for loco hauled trains to run round nor were there normally any paths even for additional dmu workings. Excursion trains were still quite popular in the 1970s but when trips were advertised to Windermere, the train could only venture as far as Oxenholme or maybe Grange-Over-Sands with passengers having to be conveyed to their final destination by fleets of buses.

DEPARTURES FROM WINDERMERE AND KENDAL
APRIL 1910

Windermere	Kendal	
–	7.00am	London Euston (arrive 1.40pm)
–	7.10am	Oxenholme
8.00am	8.14am	Oxenholme
M.O. 8.30am	8.42am	Manchester Exchange (arrive 10.26am)
–	8.50am	Preston
–	9.05am	Grange
9.15am	9.36am	Oxenholme
–	10.35am	Oxenholme
–	11.20am	Oxenholme
11.25am	11.46am	London Euston (arrive 5.40pm)
–	12.55pm	Grange
1.05pm	1.26pm	Oxenholme
S.O. –	2.20pm	Oxenholme
2.25pm	2.46pm	Oxenholme
–	3.35pm	Preston
–	3.50pm	Grange
4.20pm	4.37pm	Manchester Victoria (arrive 7.00pm)
–	5.40pm	Oxenholme
–	5.50pm	Grange
5.50pm	6.11pm	Oxenholme
6.45pm	7.06pm	Manchester Exchange (arrive 9.40pm)
–	7.45pm	Grange
9.00pm	9.18pm	Preston
SUNDAYS		
5.45pm	6.04pm	Oxenholme

M.O. – Mondays only
S.O. – Saturdays only

There are now very few special passenger trains on BR so the lack of run round facilities is less of a drawback.

In the summer of 1992, a class 142 was shuttling up and down the branch 16 times each weekday and 11 times on Sundays trying to give as many main line connections as possible.

The status of the Windermere service was raised with the May 1994 timetable. This has a 156 running every two hours from Manchester Airport through to Windermere, the unit then performing a return trip to Oxenholme and back before setting off again for Manchester Airport. In total there are now 14 departures daily from Windermere at more or less hourly intervals from 06.55 until 20.40 with a late service at 22.35 on Fridays and Saturdays only in Summer. This includes five through trains to Manchester Airport. On Sundays there are nine departures of which just one goes through to Manchester Airport. Most of the Airport trains omit stops at Staveley and Burneside.

In the mid 1980s, the track was terminated just short of the train shed at Windermere Station which has been converted into a supermarket. A new ticket office and waiting facility was built alongside the remaining bit of platform. Kendal station has also been redeveloped for non-railway use. The

A grimy 'Britannia' class 4-6-2 trundles south through Oxenholme in March 1965. The Windermere branch platform is to the left under the roof.

(Peter Sunderland)

'Black Five' 4-6-0 No. 45326 prepares to leave Windermere with a local in March 1965. *(Peter Sunderland)*

imposing building there has been restored to a high standard for the benefit of a doctors' surgery, a pharmacy and a firm of chartered accountants. The subway is now used for cars to gain access to the hotel car park which lies below the site of the demolished up platform

Remaining railway business at Kendal is done at the Windermere end of the former down platform where there is a passenger shelter but no information of any kind. A timetable poster is displayed about 100 yards away by the entrance to the approach road which is itself barred to all except railway owned vehicles. With nearby parking restrictions, it is very difficult for passengers to be deposited or met by car.

During 1984, BR considered electrifying the Windermere branch but nothing came of it. The present diesel trains are travelling 'under the wires' for more than two thirds of their $95\frac{3}{4}$ mile trip to Manchester Airport. The question may arise again in conjunction with proposals to bridge the gap in the wires between Manchester and Wigan. However, with the current level of investment in British Railways almost non-existent, nothing is likely to happen for many years.

'Britannia' class 4-6-2 No. 70027 'Rising Star' near Staveley in charge of the 8.10 Windermere to Manchester Exchange on 12 April 1966 during the last week of operation of what had been 'The Windermere Express'.
(John Marshall)

The 2.40pm from Oxenholme arrives at the 'new' Windermere terminus on 17 October 1988. The train is at about the same spot as the 'Black Five' on the previous page but on the opposite side of the island platform.
(Tom Heavyside)

Stations on the Windermere branch have been much rationalised since destaffing and track singling. Kendal looking towards Oxenholme in June 1964. The only facility now is a small shelter on the bare right hand platform near to where the van is parked.

(Peter E. Baughan)

Burneside looking towards Windermere in June 1964.

(Peter E. Baughan)

Staveley looking towards Oxenholme in September 1968.

(Peter E. Baughan)

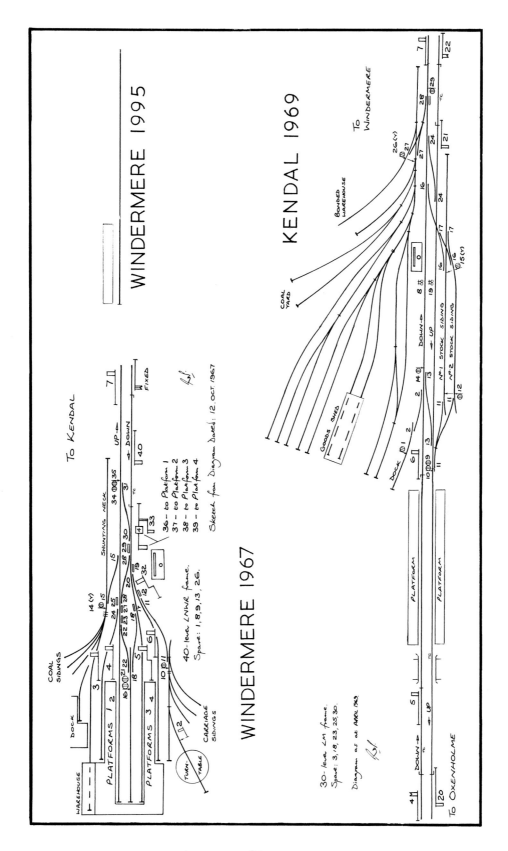

WINDERMERE 1995

WINDERMERE 1967

KENDAL 1969

39

Shipping Services

Ramsden Dock Station about 1907. 'Lady Margaret' (front) and 'Lady Evelyn' (back), both of the Furness Railway, 'Duchess of Devonshire' and 'City of Belfast', of the Barrow Steam Navigation Company and 'Lune' jointly owned by the LNWR and Lancashire & Yorkshire Railway.   *(Sankey Collection)*

Isle of Man and Ireland

The stone jetty at Morecambe had its limitations and the Midland Railway looked to a deal with the Furness in order to secure better port facilities for its Belfast steamers. Agreement was reached in 1862 that the two companies would promote jointly a 9½ mile connecting line from Wennington to Carnforth. Opened in 1867, the Furness & Midland Joint Line gave direct access from the Midland system onto the Furness and allowed the transfer of the Irish sailings from Morecambe to Piel.

The following year the Barrow Steam Navigation Company was formed bringing together the interests of the Midland and Furness Railways and those of James Little & Co. who operated the paddle steamer 'Herald' between Piel and Douglas, Isle of Man.

Piel remained the cross channel terminal until 1881 when services were transferred to a new deep water landing stage at Ramsden Dock. This eventually had its own railway station with one covered platform and a short bay, completed in 1885. Until then, trains used temporary facilities to connect with the Isle of Man and Irish boats which transferred to there from 1 June and 1 October 1881 respectively.

On 1 September 1904 the Midland Railway opened its own port at Heysham with sailings to Douglas and Belfast. The Furness tried unsuccessfully to obtain an injunction to prevent the Midland from withdrawing from the Barrow agreement. In the event the Midland bought out its

partners in the Barrow Steam Navigation Company and maintained a Barrow to Belfast sailing three days a week until the outbreak of the First World War.

In 1910 the boat train left Ramsden Dock at 6.50am, Tuesdays, Thursdays and Saturdays proceeding via Barrow Central, all stations to Carnforth and reaching Leeds at 10.42am. In the other direction it still retained some pretence as an express leaving Leeds Wellington each weekday at 5.37pm with mandatory stops only at Hellifield, Carnforth, Ulverston and Barrow Central where it terminated on the alternate days when there was no sailing. It slipped a coach at Grange and made a number of request stops including Furness Abbey 'to set down from beyond Carnforth on informing the guard at Carnforth and by signal to take up for Belfast only'.

The Furness Railway and James Little & Co maintained a thrice weekly summer only service between Ramsden Dock and Douglas until 1914. After the war there were only occasional excursions. 'Bradshaw' for April 1910 shows two sailings (per month) by the Isle of Man Steam Packet Company between Whitehaven and Ramsey. These also disappeared at the outbreak of war except for the occasional special.

The continuing association of Barrow with Irish Sea passenger shipping was mainly in the building of ships, laying them up for the winter and sometimes scrapping them.

The Bristol Channel steamer 'Gwalia', built 1905, was purchased by the Furness Railway in 1910 and later renamed 'Lady Moyra'. It is seen at Ramsden Dock still carrying its old name.
(*Sankey Collection*)

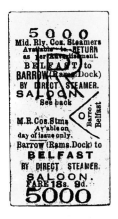

'Lady Moyra' worked on the Barrow to Fleetwood service each summer until 1914 when it was requisitioned. After the War it joined the Campbell fleet on the South Coast as the 'Brighton Belle'. It was sunk at Dunquerque in 1940.
(*Peter E. Baughan Collection*)

After the First World War, Barrow saw only occasional passenger sailings. The Isle of Man Steam Packet Company's 'Tynwald' is seen at Ramsden Dock working an excursion to Douglas in July 1964.
(*Peter Sunderland*)

Across Morecambe Bay

Early ferry services from Fleetwood to Piel were joined by ships of the Midland Railway from Morecambe following that company's takeover of 'Little' North Western Railway in 1852. These routes declined after the completion of the rail link to Barrow in 1857 and disappeared by 1869.

A Barrow to Fleetwood service was revived by the Furness Railway on a seasonal basis in August 1900. The crossing took 75 minutes and was aimed primarily at holidaymakers on the Fylde Coast who could reach Fleetwood either by train or on the newly opened Blackpool & Fleetwood Tramway. The Furness Railway offered a programme of 20 circular tours of the Lake District. Some of these were available in connection with the morning arrival at Ramsden Dock whence a train took patrons on to Furness Abbey, Greenodd or Lakeside as appropriate.

One possibility was the No. 1 tour involving train to Lakeside, steamer to Ambleside, horse drawn charabanc to Coniston and train back to Ramsden Dock for the evening departure to Fleetwood. Total fare from Blackpool was 8 shillings third class or 12 shillings first class (say about £25 and £37.50 at 1994 prices). Food extra.

Another extra was that you could have your photograph taken by Edward Sankey, official Furness Railway photographer. He travelled out on the first trip from Barrow, photographed passengers coming from Fleetwood, spent the afternoon in his dark room and tried to sell prints on the way back.

There was also traffic originating at Barrow for Fleetwood. On 6 September 1913, Barrow Football Club were away to Fleetwood. Both 'Lady Mora' and 'Lady Evelyn' sailed with full loads. The Furness Railway tug 'Walney' was pressed into service and photographed by Edward Sankey so heavily

overloaded that passengers are seen standing on the outside of the rails (*Maritime Heritage: Barrow & Morecambe Bay* by Raymond Sankey).

The cross bay sailings were another casualty of the First World War. Ramsden Dock Station fell into disuse and was demolished in 1936.

The paddle tug 'Walney' had limited passenger accommodation and sometimes helped out on the Fleetwood service. Built in 1904, it served at Barrow until 1930 after which the LMS transferred it to Scotland, where it survived until 1952.
(Sankey Collection)

Barrow in Furness Tramways

The street tramway era reached Barrow in 1885 with the inauguration on 11 July of a compact network of lines radiating from the Town Hall to the Abbey, to the steelworks and to Roose. The Abbey route also served the Central Station.

A further line opened to Ramsden Dock Station on 28 July 1886 following completion of the High Level Bridge. This brought the total route mileage to 5½. All lines were laid to a gauge of 4 foot in the centre of the road. The track was single with frequent passing loops. Eight steam locomotives were supplied by Kitson of Leeds together with eight double deck carriages.

The Barrow in Furness Tramways Co Ltd went into liquidation in 1898 but the system was purchased by the British Electric Traction Co Ltd who brought in some additional locos and carriages. These were only temporary pending electrification.

Before this change could happen, the bulk of the fleet was lost in a fire at the Salthouse Road Depot on 27 June 1902. Operation was suspended until 8 August when a reduced service was reintroduced. This continued until 13 July 1903 when all lines closed for the duration of electrification work.

The short branch to the steelworks was discarded but the Abbey and Roose lines reopened with electric traction on 6 February 1904. The Ramsden Dock line recommenced operation on 29 June.

At the end of October 1904, a branch opened to Walney Ferry, the departure point of the steam ferry to Walney Island. This line was extended to Biggar Bank on 4 August 1911 with the opening of the lifting bridge onto Walney Island. There was double track on the bridge with centre poles supporting the overhead.

With this extension, the electric network totalled 6½ route miles, almost all single track. A total of 11 single deck and 11 open top double deck trams were built for the Barrow system between 1903 and 1915. Two open top trailers were added in 1917.

Tram No. 7, built for the opening of the electric system in 1904. Of the seven vehicles of this type, four were scrapped in 1919 but one survived to the closure in 1932.
(Ian L. Cormack/Roy Brook Collection)

In 1920, the tramways were purchased by Barrow Corporation who replaced some of the fleet with single deck cars purchased, and regauged, from Southport and Sheffield. Then during the following year, they purchased 12 new single deckers.

The system closed on 5 April 1932, the Corporation having purchased 18 additional motor buses as an alternative to renewing the tramway infrastructure.

CENTRE PAGE PHOTOGRAPHS

Left Upper Coniston terminus on 16 February 1958. Being a winter Sunday, the loco is tucked away in the shed behind the camera but the push-pull set is just visible under the station roof. *(G.W. Morrison)*

Left Lower Camping coaches offered affordable if basic accommodation. M012340M is seen in the yard at Bassenthwaite Lake Station on 3 May 1958. *(J.C.W. Halliday)*

Right Upper 'Raven', the larger of the two Ullswater steamers awaits departure from Pooley Bridge on 19 August 1978. *(Martin Bairstow)*

Right Lower 'River Irt' waits at Irton Road for an uphill train to pass on 11 September 1993. Since its 1973 rebuild, this loco has assumed a quite different appearance, more 'narrow gauge' than 'miniature' thanks mainly to larger cab and chimney. *(Martin Bairstow)*

The Coniston Branch

41217 prepares to leave Coniston for Foxfield on 6 July 1957.   (J.C.W. Halliday)

The 9½ mile branch left the Cumbrian Coast Line at Foxfield but there had been no station or junction at Foxfield when the route from Kirkby to Broughton in Furness opened in February 1848. Foxfield appeared on 1 August 1858 when the direct connection to the Whitehaven & Furness Junction Railway opened leaving Broughton at the end of a short branch. Ten months later, the terminus at Broughton was closed in favour of a through station on the extension to Coniston.

The railway had been drawn first to Broughton and then to Coniston itself by copper. The Coniston Railway was incorporated in August 1857. Capital was subscribed equally by the Furness Railway and by the owners of the Coniston copper mines.

The line opened to passenger traffic on 18 June 1859 but not for freight until the following year when a short extension was brought into use to Copper Mines Wharf. The Coniston Railway was worked by the Furness who took it over completely in 1862.

The branch began at Foxfield, almost at sea level but north of Broughton it climbed at a maximum of 1 in 49 to reach a summit of 345 feet, the highest point on the Furness Railway, between Woodland and Torver. Beyond Torver there were attractive views over Coniston Water until the handsome terminus was reached above the town at Coniston.

No sooner had the Railway opened than the copper mines moved into decline leaving the branch dependent on passenger traffic and a modest amount of general freight.

As a passenger line, the Coniston branch suffered the major disadvantage of connecting into the main line at Foxfield rather than at Ulverston. Had it not been for the copper trade, it is possible to imagine a line being built, slightly later perhaps, utilising the Lakeside branch as far as Greenodd then running up the Crake Valley and alongside Coniston Water to a terminus nearer the Lake and more convenient for the town. A direct line from Ulverston to Coniston would have been less than 15 miles in length. The distance via Barrow was 31 miles with a journey taking anything from 1 hour 30 to 1 hour 50 minutes depending on the connecting times at Barrow and Foxfield.

'Bradshaw' for April 1910 shows four return trips along the branch. Normally these will have been operated by one of the two steam railcars built by the Furness Railway in 1905, if necessary hauling a four wheel trailer.

Generally speaking, the branch train was so timed that, on arrival at Foxfield, it would shunt out of the way whilst trains called in both directions on the 'main line'. Then it would come back into the platform to begin its return journey down the branch.

Passengers board the branch train at Foxfield on 6 July 1957. 41217 will propel the two coaches to Coniston.
(J.C.W. Halliday)

Broughton Station looking towards Coniston on its last day open to passengers. The photographer is standing on the staggered wooden platform built in 1903 to serve the loop line. Trains for Foxfield normally used the main platform involving right hand running.
(J.C.W. Halliday)

However, the first and last weekday trips were slightly more complicated as the up and down 'main line' trains did not meet at Foxfield. The branch train arrived at 8.05am to connect with the Whitehaven to Barrow service (depart 8.12). It then left at 8.15 for Broughton coming back to Foxfield at 8.45. As soon as the Barrow to Whitehaven train had left at 8.51, it set off again back to Coniston thus giving Barrow to Coniston and Whitehaven to Broughton connections in both directions. The same principle was applied with the tea-time service except that the westbound trains were only to and from Millom.

The railcars were withdrawn by 1918 but push – pull operation was employed during the later LMS and BR periods.

The summer timetable was quite comprehensive during the 1930s. 'Bradshaw' for July 1938 shows no fewer than 11 trains each way Mondays to Fridays with 14 on Saturdays and 6 on Sundays. Prestige train of the day was a through working from Blackpool Central to Coniston Mondays to Fridays, out in the morning, returning from Coniston at 6pm. This ran via the Dalton loop in both directions. The corresponding Saturday train was through from Morecambe Promenade via Barrow outward but via the Dalton loop on the return.

BR continued to offer a respectable service during the 1950s. 'Bradshaw' for April 1957 shows eight trips each way on weekdays though with no Sunday trains outside the peak summer months. Traffic must have been almost entirely local. A journey from Carnforth took 2¼ hours whilst poor

Depart Foxfield	Depart Coniston
8.55am	7.35am
11.55am	11.00am
3.20pm	2.30pm
6.15pm	4.25pm
Sundays	**Sundays**
10.00am	9.10am
7.20pm	6.30pm

connections made it almost impractical to reach Coniston from points further afield.

In 1958, BR claimed that they could save £16,000 per annum (say £250,000 at today's prices) by withdrawing the steam push – pull service. No thought was given to making any economies in signalling, station staff nor to replacing the steam trains with diesel units.

The last passenger train ran on 4 October 1958 to be replaced by a service of Ribble buses, subsidised by British Railways and supposedly running in connection with the trains but without any mention in the railway timetable. The buses employed had to be of limited size pending construction of a number of passing places on the tortuous road.

Goods trains continued for another 3½ years with a pick up running three times a week though traffic north of Broughton was very light.

Broughton, Woodland and Torver stations remain as private dwellings but the site of Coniston station has been cleared to make a car park.

Steam railcar and trailer in Coniston Station. The engine compartment is at the far end of the railcar which seated 12 first and 36 third class passengers. There was a second driving position at the rear end of the railcar and one at the end of the trailer so it could travel either way with or without the trailer.

(Real Photographs, Courtesy Rex Kennedy)

The push-pull set leaves Woodland for Coniston, almost for the last time on Saturday 4 October 1958.
(J.C.W. Halliday)

The main building at Woodland still exists as a private dwelling. In its operational days it combined the functions of railway station and Post office.
(J C W Halliday)

Ivatt 2-6-2T No. 41221 has brought the push-pull into Coniston. The small engine shed is visible through the station.

(J. Davenport)

Coniston was visited by the 'Furness Railtour' on 27 August 1961. 4F 0-6-0 No. 44347 afforded patrons a last chance to travel on the branch.
(J.C.W. Halliday)

The passenger entrance to Coniston Station.
(J C W Halliday)

The Lakeside Branch

Lakeside on a Sunday in July 1959 with 42581 on the 7.20pm to Barrow and a dmu on an excursion from Leeds.   *(Peter Sunderland)*

The Furness Railway reached the southern tip of Lake Windermere with an eight mile branch from Plumpton Junction on its Carnforth to Barrow main line. It was a most scenic branch running through the Leven Valley. Closed by British Railways, it would have made an excellent preserved railway but, sadly, part of the route was sequestrated in the cause of road improvements leaving just an isolated operation over three miles between Haverthwaite and Lakeside.

The River Leven flows out of Lake Windermere and into Morecambe Bay. It is only a short river which, once it reaches Greenodd, widens into an estuary. When the Leven Viaduct was built carrying the Ulverston & Lancaster Railway, it was obliged to include an opening span in order to preserve navigation to the small port of Greenodd.

When the Furness Railway sought powers in 1863 for a two mile branch to Greenodd, it was able to buy off the obligation to keep the opening span on the Leven Viaduct. In return for losing their port, the traders of Greenodd were offered rail access to the Ulverston Canal basin at favourable rates.

Powers were obtained in 1866 to continue the Greenodd branch as far as Newby Bridge which was the limit of navigation for the small steamers then operating on Windermere. Work began, but whilst this was going on, it was decided to extend the branch beyond Newby Bridge so as to establish a rail/ship interchange at Lakeside on Windermere itself thus avoiding ships having to navigate the River Leven to reach Newby Bridge. This decision later permitted larger vessels to be built for service on the Lake.

Goods traffic began as far as Greenodd on 18 March 1869 and to Newby Bridge on 23 April. Then on 1 June 1869, the entire branch opened for passengers and freight through to Lakeside.

Principal customers were the gunpowder works at Low Wood and Black Beck. Both these had their own rail access. The pre existing 3ft 6in gauge system at Low Wood was extended across the River Leven to reach Haverthwaite goods yard. There were two reversals on the climb up from the river to Haverthwaite. Motive power was provided by horses, the gunpowder works not offering a suitable environment for steam locomotives. The works closed in 1935.

Black Beck was served by a two mile standard gauge branch, also worked by horses. This diverged in a northerly direction between Greenodd and Haverthwaite, the ground frame being released by a key issued with the single line token. Black Beck works closed in 1928.

Other freight on the branch included ore going into the Backbarrow ironworks and pig iron coming out. The works had a private siding at the Lakeside end of Haverthwaite goods yard. There was timber from the local coppice industry, some of it going out as pit props. There were coal deliveries to all stations including fuel for the steamers at Lakeside

The branch offered a year round passenger service from its opening until 1938. Winter traffic was never heavy and in 1905 the Furness Railway experimented with two 48 seat steam 'railmotors' for this and the Coniston branch. An unstaffed halt was opened at Newby Bridge to coincide with introduction of the 'railmotor'.

'Bradshaw' for April 1910 shows six departures from Ulverston at 9.15 and 10.45am, 1.00, 2.25, 5.00 and 7.05pm. All but the last have steamer connections at Lakeside for Bowness and Ambleside and most are shown as having a bus connection thence to Grasmere.

The basic service was augmented by seasonal extra timetabled trains as well as excursions.

'Bradshaw' for July 1938 shows a similar pattern of trains between Ulverston and Lakeside as in 1910 but there are two additional trains in a morning running through from Morecambe to Lakeside via the Leven Curve.

This curve afforded direct access onto the branch from the east avoiding reversal at Ulverston. It was lifted during the First World War then reinstated only to suffer the same fate, again temporarily, during the Second World War. It closed for the third time in 1952.

The passenger service between Ulverston and Lakeside was withdrawn on 26 September 1938 with the intention that it should continue in Summer only thereafter. This happened during 1939 and 1940 but there was only a token operation in 1941.

Passenger trains resumed on 3 June 1946 again on a seasonal basis. Greenodd and Haverthwaite stations had remained open for passengers in summer and for parcels all year round but they

Plumpton Junction seen from a dmu which has reversed there in order to take the Lakeside branch, the Leven Curve having been lifted.
(Peter Sunderland)

Passing through the closed station at Greenodd in July 1959. The viaduct which will take the train across a narrow point in the Leven Estuary is visible to the right of the signal box. (Peter Sunderland)

closed at the end of the 1946 operation.

Much of the track was relaid in the early 1960s but then came the Beeching Report in March 1963. A line with only seasonal excursion traffic had no chance. The last regular passenger train, a dmu, pulled out of Lakeside at 7.45 on the evening of Sunday 5 September 1965.

Freight to Lakeside had ceased in April 1964 but there was still enough traffic at Haverthwaite to justify a pick up goods on Mondays, Wednesdays and Fridays which was steam hauled to the end. This came in April 1967 when the ironworks at Haverthwaite closed.

A special brake van trip ran all the way to Lakeside on 2 September 1967 behind 'Black Five' No 45134. This gave a handful of enthusiasts and well wishers what was expected to be their last look at the branch.

Preservation

Moves aimed at preserving the Lakeside branch began during 1967. The Lakeside Railway Estates Co Ltd, formed in June that year was interested both in the operation of the branch from Plumpton Junction to Lakeside and in the recreation of a main line steam depot at Carnforth.

Meanwhile a supporting organisation, the Lakeside Railway Society was created by a group which had got together some years earlier as the Lancaster Railway Circle.

Ivatt 2-6-0 No 46441 had been purchased privately for preservation and it was expected that this might operate on the branch. In January 1968, it was joined at Carnforth by two Fairburn 2-6-4 tank engines. All three locos had been built after 1948 and were representative of types which had worked to Lakeside during the BR period. The Society made its own contribution by purchasing 0-4-0ST 'Caliban' from Courtaulds at Preston.

BR had threatened to begin removing track in September 1967 but were persuaded not to do so in view of the possibility of selling the branch.

However, BR were obliged to give first option on any closed line to the local authority. Early in 1968, the Lake District Planning Board announced its intention to acquire the track bed north of Haverthwaite and convert it into a footpath. The Society tried to negotiate with the Planning Board but made little impact at first. During the Summer of 1968, they raised a petition with over 12,600 signatures and in September were able to reach a compromise. The Planning Board would purchase the track bed of the Haverthwaite to Lakeside section which was wide enough for double track. They would lease to the Railway Company land upon which the single track was laid and would establish alongside it their footpath – which in the event has never materialised.

That hurdle overcome, 1968 closed with a Society membership of 300 and much optimism about the future. The Lakeside Railway Estates Company held its first open day at Carnforth Shed on Sunday 1

Greenodd Station, 4 October 1958. The building was sacrificed in the cause of road widening.

(J.C.W. Halliday)

June 1969 when 3,000 people visited. It had been hoped to run specials on the Lakeside branch itself on this centenary day but BR turned down the idea as was their wont with all similar preservation schemes.

There was worse news than that. During the Summer of 1969, the Lancashire County Council decided to exercise its option to acquire two bits of the line south of Haverthwaite in order to effect road improvements.

This killed the prospect of preserving the entire branch. It also split supporters into two camps, some preferring to abandon the branch line in favour of developing Carnforth, others wishing to concentrate effort on the three miles between Haverthwaite and Lakeside. The two factions fell out and in June 1970, the Lakeside Railway Estates Company told the Lakeside Railway Society to remove its property from Carnforth.

This they did taking advantage of the opportunity to do so by rail prior to the Plumpton Junction – Haverthwaite section being demolished.

On Wednesday 14 October 1970, class 24 No D5100 left York at 3.30am hauling eight carriages which had been purchased by the new Lakeside & Haverthwaite Railway Company. It reached Haverthwaite at 10.50 and set off back light engine. At Carnforth it passed class 08 No D3200 at the head of 'The Lakeside & Haverthwaite Harbinger' which comprised the two Fairburn tanks, 'Caliban' and a mess van.

46441 remained at Carnforth, its owner preferring, evidently, the potential of eventual main line operation rather than the constraints of a three mile stretch of isolated track.

There were in total four more movements over the Plumpton Junction to Haverthwaite section including that on 26 November 1970 which brought 'black five' No 44806 from Accrington. This was the loco whose brief appearance at Helmshore over the previous August Bank Holiday Weekend had provided a temporary boost in morale to the struggling East Lancashire Railway Preservation Society.

The last stock movement saw class 25 No D5194 deliver a brake second coach on 7 May 1971. A few weeks later, the track was lifted leaving Haverthwaite permanently cut off from the BR system.

Before operation could commence between Lakeside and Haverthwaite, there remained the bureaucratic procedures which have effected all preservation schemes. First BR had to apply for a statutory order bringing the line within the orbit of the Light Railways Act, 1896. Then a second order was required transferring the operating powers to the new owners.

By the Autumn of 1971, the Lakeside & Haverthwaite Company felt confident that matters were sufficiently advanced to permit services to begin at Easter 1972. Unfortunately, but in common with other preservationists, they failed to appreciate how long these things take. Easter 1973 was also

'Black Five' 4-6-0 No. 44877 climbing from Haverthwaite towards Newby Bridge.   (D.J. Mitchell)

missed but, finally, on Wednesday 2 May 1973, the 'Reopening Special' was drawn out of Lakeside Station by the two Fairburn tanks.

Since then the Railway has operated a seasonal service generally coinciding with the period of operation of the Windermere Steamers.

The 1993 season ran from 3 April to 31 October except that there were no Monday to Friday trains during the last two weeks of April although the steamers ran on these dates. The timetable offers between five and seven return trips generally offering good connections at Lakeside. Through tickets are available to Bowness and Ambleside.

The Railway participates in such ventures as 'The Lakeland Link' whereby passengers from Ambleside or Bowness can book a full days outing involving steamer to Lakeside, train to Haverthwaite, bus to Holker Hall for a 2½ hour stay and then back to Lakeside.

Holker Hall, which now combines a stately home with a motor museum, was one of the attractions featured amongst the 'Twenty Coach and Steam Yacht Tours' offered by the Furness Railway 90 years ago.

The difference is that the Railway then was capable of bringing people into the Lake District and still could have done so but for the demolition of a mere 4½ miles of track between Plumpton Junction and Haverthwaite.

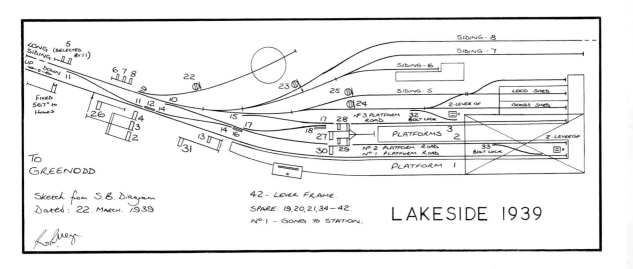

'Black Five' 4-6-0 No. 44730 exchanges tokens at Haverthwaite en route for Lakeside in 1964.

(D.J. Mitchell)

44877 has arrived at Lakeside with its 3 coach payload. The track layout has been rationalised since the 1959 visit.

(D.J. Mitchell)

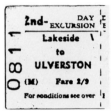

Ex Midland Railway 2F 0-6-0 No. 58123 shunting at Lakeside on a rather inclement day about 1958.

(J. Davenport)

The distinctive terminal building at Lakeside, demolished in 1969 supposedly to facilitate strengthening of the pier. 'Swan' alongside.

(Douglas Butterfield)

Jubilee class 4-6-0 No. 45559 'British Columbia' in the 'long siding' just outside Lakeside with empty stock for a return excursion to Colne in July 1959. *(Peter Sunderland)*

42073 climbing away from Haverthwaite with the 3.32pm to Lakeside on 22 July 1973. Both Fairburn tanks were built by BR in 1950/51 but at this time 42073 was turned out in LNWR livery and 42085 in Caldedonian. *(Tom Heavyside)*

Similar to BR class J94, 0-6-0ST 'Cumbria' draws the empty stock which has been stabled in the West Tunnel into Haverthwaite Station ready for the first departure to Lakeside on 19 September 1976.

(Martin Bairstow)

Lakeside Station on 19 November 1994 with a preserved Class 110 set helping to extend the operating season on Thursdays, Saturdays and Sundays until the end of the month. *(Martin Bairstow)*

The Lake Steamers

'Teal' at Bowness on 12 July 1974. 'Swan' is very similar in appearance.

(Martin Bairstow)

The introduction of the steamship coincided with the development of steam power on the railways and the two forms of transport have always been closely associated. Many railway companies became directly involved in the operation of cross channel, coastal and lake steamer services.

The first steam vessel to run on an English Lake was the 'Lady of the Lake' which appeared on Windermere in 1845. The Windermere fleet subsequently passed into the hands of the Furness Railway which also operated a ship on Coniston. Ullswater never had a direct rail link and there the steamers remained outside railway ownership.

Prior to the motor age, the ships on Windermere and Ullswater provided a general service for passengers, mail and even a certain amount of freight. In more recent times they have catered for tourists on a seasonal basis.

Compared to a sea going ship, the life of a lake steamer is a rather tranquil affair and many of the vessels have enjoyed extreme longevity. Steam has given way almost entirely to diesel power but the ships are still commonly referred to as 'steamers'.

Windermere

Launched at Newby Bridge in 1845, the 'Lady of the Lake' was a wooden paddle steamer capable of conveying about 200 passengers. It belonged to the Windermere Steam Yacht Company which introduced a second, similar vessel, the 'Lord of the Isles' in 1846. Operating between Newby Bridge, Bowness and Ambleside, the 'Lord of the Isles' was destroyed by fire in 1850 but the 'Lady of the Lake' continued until superseded by larger vessels after 1866.

The rival Windermere Iron Steamboat Company appeared in 1849. Allied to the Kendal & Windermere Railway, it put into service two paddle steamers, the 'Firefly' and 'Dragonfly'. These operated in competition with the older company until 1858 when the two concerns amalgamated to form the Windermere United Steam Yacht Company.

The 'Rothay', launched in 1866, was probably the largest vessel which could get up the Leven to Newby Bridge. It was a paddle steamer with a rudder at each end so it did not need to turn in the river.

The 1866 Act for the Newby Bridge branch had empowered the Furness Railway to invest in the Windermere United Steam Yacht Company. Full takeover eventually followed in 1875. Meanwhile, in 1869, the branch had opened not just to Newby Bridge but to a terminus at Lakeside on Windermere itself. The steamers no longer needed to negotiate the Leven up to Newby Bridge.

Just five days after arrival of the railway, the 'Swan' was launched from the slipway at Lakeside. This was a larger vessel than those which had gone before. With capacity for over 400 passengers, it was the first of the Windermere fleet to be driven by propellers rather than paddles.

The steamer service was now effectively an extension of the Lakeside branch railway. Bowness and Ambleside were Furness stations with no tracks.

The 'Raven', which entered service in 1871, looked after the freight service. It carried goods from Lakeside to various destinations along the shores of Windermere, also serving as an icebreaker in winter. The arrival of the 'Cygnet' and 'Teal' in 1879 allowed most of the pre-railway fleet to be scrapped. The last of these, the 'Rothay' was withdrawn in 1891 upon delivery of the 'Tern'. With capacity for 600 passengers, this was the largest vessel up to that time and is the oldest of the present day fleet. It was

joined in 1900 by the 'Swift' which is even larger with capacity for over 700 passengers.

In 1907 the Furness Railway purchased the 'Britannia', a private yacht which had been built in 1879. It was used as a 'Directors' Saloon' and also for private parties but was withdrawn during the First World War and scrapped shortly afterwards.

'Bradshaw' for April 1910 shows a basic winter service of five sailings each way Sundays excepted all connecting with trains to and from Ulverston.

All year round steamer operation ceased in 1920 when the Furness Railway acquired two single deck buses from the Great Western with which to run a replacement service between Newby Bridge and Ambleside. The railway buses ran for two winters after which the function passed to the local bus operator.

The freight steamer 'Raven' was withdrawn in 1922 but it has survived and is now in the

On board passenger facilities have improved somewhat since 1920. 'Swift' is pulling away from Lakeside passing the equally spartan 'Cygnet'.
(Sankey Collection)

'Swift' at Ambleside on 12 July 1974.

(Martin Bairstow)

Windermere Steamboat Museum. In 1924 the 'Cygnet' was converted from steam to diesel propulsion with mixed success. It was disposed of during the LMS period.

The level of summer traffic was sufficient for the LMS to invest in new tonnage. The 'Teal' and 'Swan' appeared in 1936 and 1938 respectively replacing the earlier vessels of the same name. Both were 251 tons diesel ships with space for 800 passengers on their three decks. They were made in Barrow and conveyed by rail to Lakeside in sections. Their arrival brought the fleet up to its final tally of four vessels. The 'Tern' and 'Swift' were converted to diesel power in 1957/8.

From 1970, British Railways operated its fleet of ships through a subsidiary company, Sealink (UK) Ltd. In 1985 Sealink was privatised being acquired by Sea Containers which revived the name Windermere Iron Steamboat Company. The 'Swift' has not run since 1982 and is currently moored at Lakeside as a floating exhibition centre.

'Swan', 'Teal' and 'Tern' have been refurbished. With stricter safety regulations and higher standards expected by customers, their carrying capacity is now limited to 550 for the larger boats and 350 on the 'Tern'. They operate from Easter until the end of October with up to nine return trips scheduled each day during the high season.

The 1993 timetable urged customers: "Before paying for your ticket or booking a cruise, please ensure that you are dealing with the Windermere Iron Steamboat Company". This remark was clearly aimed at the rival Bowness Bay Boating Company Ltd which had, for years, operated a more frequent service between Bowness and Ambleside using smaller craft.

For 1994, the two services are amalgamated. The traditional steamers operate almost exactly as before whilst the Bowness Bay Company vessels appear in the same timetable so as to offer a combined frequency of up to three boats an hour between Bowness and Ambleside.

During the early and late season, one of the smaller vessels makes an early afternoon trip to Lakeside filling a gap in the previous off peak timetable. Otherwise the southern part of the lake remains the preserve of the 'Swan', 'Teal' and 'Tern'.

'Tern' arriving at Bowness on 12 September 1973. It has since been rebuilt with more superstructure including a bridge near the front which radically alters its appearance.
(Stuart Baker)

The former goods vessel 'Raven' preserved at the Windermere Steamboat Museum which is located about 3/4 mile north of Bowness.

(Martin Bairstow)

'Miss Lakeland' passing Storrs en route from Lakeside to Bowness on 19 November 1994, maintaining a three days per week service to the end of that month. Vessels of the Bowness Bay Boating Company also run from Bowness to Ambleside daily through the winter. Storrs was a request stop for the steamers during the LMS period.

(Martin Bairstow)

Coniston

The service on Coniston Water was instituted by a group of Furness Railway directors following opening of the branch in 1859. It was not until 1872 that the Railway Company obtained statutory powers for direct participation in the Windermere and Coniston steamships.

The 'Gondola' was ordered from Jones, Quiggin & Co of Liverpool and transported to Coniston in sections by rail. It was launched in October 1859 and commenced regular sailings the following June. The resemblance to the Venetian gondola is quite evident. The vessel carried over 200 passengers and proved sufficient for the modest traffic on Coniston for almost 50 years.

In 1908 the 'Lady of the Lake' arrived by rail in pieces from J & I Thornycroft of Southampton to be assembled at Coniston. It was similar in appearance to the 'Tern' on Windermere but smaller. Passenger capacity was 400. The 'Gondola' was relegated to be the reserve boat.

The LMS timetable for May and June 1934 shows 'Lady of the Lake' performing three return trips between the piers at Waterhead and Lake Bank. The service ran Sundays excepted commencing on Saturday 19 May, the same day that the Windermere boats began. Bus connections are shown from Greenodd Station to Lake Bank and from Waterhead (Coniston) to Ambleside on Windermere.

Sailings were interrupted at the outbreak of the Second World War and did not resume for 40 years. The 'Lady of the Lake' was broken up in 1950 but the 'Gondola' had been sold for use as a houseboat. It was eventually acquired by the National Trust in 1977 after spending a number of years submerged.

'Lady of the Lake' prior to launching at Coniston in 1903.

(Sankey Collection)

Following a public appeal, restoration was carried out to a very high standard by Vickers of Barrow. The 'Gondola' re-entered service in July 1980 and now operates from Easter until the end of October offering up to five trips per day between Coniston Pier, Park-a-Moor and Brantwood.

The majority of passengers take the 55 minute round trip from Coniston Pier though single fares are offered between the other piers. Operation can be interrupted by even modest bad weather. The 'Gondola' offers the only opportunity to travel on a steam driven 'steamer'. The sensation is quite different to that of the diesel ships on the other lakes.

A further chance to sail on Coniston is afforded by the Coniston Ferry Service which operates up to eight round trips per day using a small 'traditional timber craft'. Sailing between Coniston Pier, Waterhead, Torver, Brantwood and back to Coniston Pier, this runs every day from late March to mid November and at weekends only during the winter.

The well appointed saloon on board the 'Gondola'.
(Martin Bairstow)

The 'Gondola' departs from Coniston Pier on 16 July 1994.
(Martin Bairstow)

Ullswater

A regular service between Pooley Bridge and Glenridding was opened in 1859 by the paddle steamer 'Enterprise'.

In 1877, the Ullswater Navigation & Transit Company put into service the 'Lady of the Lake'. Built by T B Seath & Co of Rutherglen, it had a capacity for 220 passengers. It was joined in 1889 by the slightly larger 'Raven' also from T B Seath & Co. Both vessels are still in operation. They were converted from steam to diesel in 1935.

The 'Lady of the Lake' has sunk at least twice but in 1965 it was badly damaged by a fire which broke out in an adjacent workshop whilst laid up for the winter. It did not re-enter service until 1979.

Ullswater has never been directly served by rail but 'Bradshaw' used to show bus connections between Penrith Station and Pooley Bridge. The April 1910 edition shows three connecting services in each direction daily (except Sundays) between Penrith, Pooley Bridge, Howtown (by request) and Glenridding, which was then listed as Patterdale.

Fifty years later, my 'Bradshaw' for December 1960 has a table headed 'Ullswater Lake (steamer)'. No times are shown, presumably because it is winter, though there is no explanation to that effect. Nor is there any space for Penrith bus connections. The adjacent table for the Keswick line shows a footnote against Penrith: 'Station for Ullswater Lake (Pooley Bridge 5½ miles)' – very helpful.

In 1994, the ships operated from Easter to the end of October. The 'Raven' made three return trips between Glenridding, Howtown and Pooley Bridge whilst 'The Lady of the Lake' provided an additional five short workings between Glenridding and Howtown only. The frequency was lower during April and October.

Derwent Water

A fleet of passenger launches, some of them quite elderly is operated by the Keswick on Derwent Water Launch Company Ltd.

The service operates daily from March to November and at weekends through the winter. Starting from Keswick, the launches serve six other landing stages around the lake. Frequency varies from four times per day in winter up to every quarter of an hour in late July and August. Generally, alternate departures from Keswick go clockwise and anti-clockwise around the lake.

'Annie Mellor' pulls into the small landing stage at High Brandelhow on 1 September 1990.

(Martin Bairstow)

'Lady of the Lake' at Glenridding on 26 March 1989.
(Martin Bairstow)

The Cockermouth, Keswick & Penrith Railway

2-6-4T No. 42314 at Keswick with the 'Lakes Express' for London Euston on 20 August 1960.

(John Marshall)

The prime motivation for this highly scenic route across the northern Lake District lay in the carriage of freight. By 1860, West Cumberland pig iron and raw ore were required by the steel industries in Durham and Yorkshire. At the same time the available coke ovens could not convert coal mined in Cumberland. The right sort of coal had to be brought there from the Durham coalfield. A staple two-way traffic thus appeared guaranteed to the promoters of a cross country railway.

A route was already available via Maryport, Carlisle and Newcastle but in 1858, the Eden Valley Railway was authorised from Kirkby Stephen to Penrith. When this opened four years later, only the 30 mile gap between Cockermouth and Penrith remained to be filled in order to complete a shorter more southerly coast to coast route and work was already under way to that end.

The Cockermouth & Workington Railway

The western most link in the cross country chain was the 8³/4 mile Cockermouth & Workington. Authorised in 1845 and opened on 28 April 1847, this line left the Whitehaven Junction Railway by a very sharp curve at Derwent Junction, ¹/4 miles north of Workington station.

The single line was built on the cheap with 11 wooden bridges. These had to be replaced with iron structures in the early 1860s when the opportunity was also taken to widen them in anticipation of a second track being laid.

Double track was in use throughout by 1868, the work having been completed by the London & North Western Railway which absorbed both the Cockermouth & Workington and the Whitehaven Junction on 16 July 1866.

There were two branches off the Cockermouth & Workington. Both were products of the prosperity of West Cumberland industry in the 1860s and both became relatively early casualties in the twentieth century.

In 1863, the Whitehaven, Cleator & Egremont Railway obtained powers to extend northwards from its then terminus at Wright Green (known as Lamplugh after 1901) to join the Cockermouth & Whitehaven by a triangular junction at Marron. The 6¹/2 mile route opened to goods on 15 January 1866 and to passengers on 2 April. A station was provided at Marron Junction. It had an island platform after the track was doubled but was closed at the end of June 1897. Five years later the south to

Workington Station was rebuilt by the LNWR in 1886. For years the building lurked under several coats of grime but stone cleaning has restored some of its original style.

(David Beeken)

east curve at Marron was removed. Passenger services were withdrawn between Moor Row and Marron Junction in April 1931 and the line was closed to all traffic north of Rowrah in May 1954.

The Derwent Branch of the Maryport & Carlisle Railway was authorised in June 1865 and opened from Bullgill to Brigham on 1 June 1867. The Maryport & Carlisle was granted running powers under its 1865 Act westward from Brigham to Marron Junction and eastward to Cockermouth. A passenger service ran from Maryport to Cockermouth with reversals at both Bullgill and Brigham from 1 November 1866. This branch was closed to all traffic in April 1935.

The Cockermouth, Keswick & Penrith Railway

The company which was to build the 31¼ mile single line from Cockermouth to Penrith was incorporated in August 1861. It was quickly decided that the C K & P would not be an operating railway. A subsequent Act of June 1863 provided that passenger and general goods trains would be worked by the London & North Western Railway and mineral traffic by the Stockton & Darlington as successor to both the South Durham & Lancashire Union (Stainmore) and Eden Valley Railways. Soon after, the Stockton & Darlington was itself merged into the North Eastern Railway who in June 1864 obtained powers for the curve between Redhills and Eamont Junctions which would allow traffic to and from their line to avoid reversal at Penrith.

The C K & P opened to goods on 26 October 1864 and to passengers on 2 January 1865. The Redhills curve followed on 5 September 1866. This was double track leaving the C K & P on the north side then passing underneath.

The C K & P began at Cockermouth Junction, more than ¼ miles west of the original Cockermouth

Station, terminus of the line from Workington. From 1865, this became the goods depot, the route to Penrith climbing alongside at 1 in 70 in order to reach the new station, a little way to the east. At first this had only one platform adjoining the substantial stone building but by 1875 an island platform had also been provided on the south side, reached by a subway.

Bassenthwaite Lake was one of the most picturesque spots on the line. The LMS and BR stationed camping coaches here. The view eastwards was dominated by Skiddaw (3,053 feet). For three miles the line ran along the shore of the lake.

Keswick station was located on the northern edge of the town which itself stands by the shore of Derwent Water surrounded by mountains. The main station building was on the south side with subway connection to the island which was built in 1894 in place of the original eastbound platform. The 76 bedroom Keswick Hotel was built by the C K & P but sold off to an independent operator. There was direct covered access from station to hotel.

In the 3½ miles between Keswick and Threlkeld the railway negotiated the Greta Gorge. In this distance there were two short tunnels and a dozen bridges including eight underline bowstring girders as the railway crossed and recrossed the River Greta.

One mile east of Keswick a loop in the River provided the site of Briery Bobbin Mill which, from 1891, had a private siding, accessed from a ground frame. About 1922, the mill also gained a passenger platform for the benefit of employees arriving by train. The halt closed with the mill in 1958 but is still there serving as one of the points of access to 'The Railway Footpath'.

The heavy coke and ore trains, particularly the eastbound traffic climbing out of Keswick, placed a strain on the capacity of the single line. At first there were passing loops only at Cockermouth Station, Bassenthwaite Lake, Keswick and Penruddock. Redhills Junction was added with the opening of the Eamont Junction curve in 1866. Troutbeck acquired a second platform, passing loop and signal box in 1874.

Staff and ticket working was employed but in 1883 the C P & K went modern by introducing Tyer's electric tablet system between Cockermouth Junction and Cockermouth Station. The electric tablet, which had then only just been invented, was later installed right through to Penrith between 1889 and 1891.

There remained an eight mile bottleneck between Keswick and Troutbeck upon which permissive block was still being used in 1892. That is a train could be despatched without confirmation that the previous one had cleared the section. The Board of Trade applied pressure for this practice to be stopped.

In 1892 a passing loop was installed at Threlkeld along with an intermediate block post at Highgate. Double line working was then introduced in 1894 between Threlkeld and Troutbeck. It was extended to Penruddock in 1901 when the Blencow to Redhills Junction section was also doubled.

Highgate was located roughly half way between Threlkeld and Troutbeck, a remote spot a little to the east of the 12 arch Mosedale Viaduct, the largest structure on the line. Requests for a station at Highgate were consistently rejected by the C K & P until 1908 when they accepted a contribution from the County Council Education Committee to provide staggered platforms for the benefit of schoolchildren.

Opened on 17 August 1908, the halt was served once a day in each direction on school days only. No nameboards were provided in order to minimise the risk of any other customers learning about it. At one time, there were more than 20 children using the halt to reach school in Threlkeld but the facility finished at the end of the Christmas term in 1928 by which time a regular bus service had become available. The small signal box at Highgate closed in May 1931.

By now the C K & P had lost its separate identity. Never an operating company, it retained ownership of the track, stations and signalling until 1923 when the 'grouping' brought it in to the London Midland & Scottish Railway.

With the demise of the heavy freight traffic in the 1920s, the Redhills Junction to Eamont Junction curve fell into disuse after 1926 though it was not finally abandoned until June 1938. Redhills Junction box was then closed and single line working introduced between Blencow and Penrith No. 1 Box.

Passenger Train Services

In 1885, there were five weekday trains in each direction between Workington and Penrith with just one on Sundays. 25 years later in 1910 the number had risen to six on weekdays but still only one on Sundays. There was an extra train, including one on Sundays between Workington and Cockermouth. The latter town also had a service of six trains (two on Sundays) operated by the Maryport & Carlisle Railway. Most of these were through Maryport but some required a change at Bullgill.

The basic year round service was supplemented in mid-summer by additional trains including some conveying through carriages to further afield. Having previously resisted pressure from the C K & P, the LNWR first introduced a through train from Keswick to London during the summer of 1886.

The service was reduced towards the end of the First World War leaving a basic service of only four trains each way, weekdays only by 1918.

Ivatt 2-6-0 No. 46432 crossing the River Derwent on the final approach to Workington with the 1.50pm from Penrith on 20 July 1963. It is viewed through the front of the 3.20pm dmu which is about to turn onto the Keswick line at Derwent Junction.
(John Birkbeck)

The 9.05am Carlisle to Workington via Penrith pauses at Cockermouth on 7 November 1963.

(Peter E. Baughan)

46426 and 46458 passing through Bassenthwaite Lake with the 'Solway Ranger' tour on 13 June 1964.

(G.W. Morrison)

The station master at Braithwaite has exchanged tokens with the driver of this Workington bound dmu. There was no passing loop here nor a signal box, just a four lever ground frame on the other side of the track near the level crossing.
(Peter E. Baughan)

The 11.56am from Workington to Penrith approaching Keswick on 20 July 1963. No. 2 signal box to the left. The 1954 built 'Derby Lightweight' sets comprised a motor coach and a driving trailer. They were all withdrawn by 1969.
(John Birkbeck)

They were replaced on this line by units of class 108, also built at Derby, one of which is seen approaching Penruddock from Keswick on 4 March 1972, the last day of service. They looked smart enough in the original lined green but the all over blue livery did absolutely nothing for them.
(Keith Preston)

A summary of eastbound departures is set out opposite for the Summer of 1938. The 9.00 from Workington was 'The Lakes Express' which also picked up portions from Windermere and Blackpool. It reached the capital at 4.47pm (SX) and 5.20pm (SO).

The Sunday trains ran only in mid-summer. The Glasgow working, which conveyed a restaurant car, ran via Dumfries to reach St Enoch terminus at 10.46pm. It had set off from there at 9.55 in the morning offering five hours in Keswick to anyone who made the full day trip. The Newcastle train, which only managed a buffet car, brought LNER corridor stock to Keswick each summer Sunday.

The 1953 Summer timetable shows six eastbound departures from Keswick augmented by the 'Lakes Express' between 13 July and 12 September and by a through train to Manchester Victoria on Saturday mornings during the same period. There are no Sunday trains shown.

Departures from C K & P Line (Eastbound) July 1938

Workington	Cockermouth	Keswick	
6.45am	7.10am	7.43am	Penrith
7.45	8.15	—	Keswick
8.26	8.53	9.30	Penrith
9.00	9.25	9.59	London Euston
—	—	SO 10.10	Leeds
9.58	10.30	11.05	Penrith (Carlisle SX)
10.50	11.21	11.55	Penrith
SO 11.50	SO 12.17pm	—	Keswick
SO 12.30pm	—	—	Cockermouth
SO 12.50	—	—	Cockermouth
2.10	2.37	3.15pm	Penrith
—	—	SX 3.55	Penrith
3.52	4.19	—	Cockermouth
—	—	SO 5.10	Penrith
5.34	6.01	6.40	Penrith
6.50	7.20	7.58	Penrith
8.40	—	—	Cockermouth
SO 9.15	—	—	Cockermouth
Sundays			
1.21pm	1.48pm	—	Keswick
—	—	6.55pm	Glasgow St Enoch
—	—	7.10	Newcastle

SO = Saturdays only
SX = Saturdays excepted

Modernisation Then Closure

Diesel multiple units first appeared on the Keswick line in January 1955, part of a scheme which also involved the routes from Carlisle to Silloth and to Workington via Maryport. The twin powered 'Derby Lightweight' sets scored some success in attracting additional traffic. They were faster, cleaner and cheaper to operate. They also offered a much better view. A number of trains started running through to Carlisle. The diesels also brought the reopening of Blencow Station and the reintroduction of Sunday trains including the through working from Newcastle which was steam hauled until 1960 and dmu thereafter.

Unfortunately, that was just about the extent of the revolution which accompanied dieselisation. Old thinking continued and by 1959 there were suggestions that the line might be closed because it was losing £50,000 per annum.

Nothing happened until 1963 when the Beeching Report recommended that the entire route from Workington to Penrith be swept away. All goods facilities were withdrawn with effect from 1 June 1964 except for access to the quarries at Flusco and Blencow.

A proposal to withdraw all passenger services was put through the usual TUCC procedure. The matter then passed to the Minister of Transport who decreed in the Autumn of 1965 that the route should be closed west of Keswick but retained thence to Penrith in view of the hardship which would be suffered by users were that section to close also.

The last trains ran between Workington and Keswick on 16 April 1966 leaving a service of six trains each way between Keswick and Penrith, some of them extended to Carlisle. 'The Lakes Express' had run for the last time at the end of the previous summer timetable.

During 1967, the Transport Minister, Barbara Castle, introduced a 'white paper' which proposed 'inter alia' to fix the size of the BR network at a level greater than that proposed in the Beeching Report. Penrith to Keswick was one of a number of lines which were to be retained as 'basic railways' whereby costs would be reduced as an alternative to closure.

On 3 December 1967, the four remaining signal boxes were closed at Blencow, Penruddock, Threlkeld and Keswick No. 1. Except at the two quarries, all points, loops and sidings were taken out of use and the entire branch from Penrith No. 1 Box (the erstwhile Keswick Junction) to the buffer stop at Keswick Station was worked on the 'one engine in steam' principle.

From 1 July 1968, all five branch stations became unstaffed, no distinction being drawn between the remote intermediate stations and Keswick itself.

Most lines which had managed to survive this far were then able to remain open in what gradually became a less hostile environment. There were, however, a few exceptions and Penrith to Keswick was one of them. Another was Bury to Rawtenstall whose fate is described in *The East Lancashire Railway*.

Exactly the same thing happened at Keswick. Underpinning Barbara Castle's plan to stabilise the BR network was a system of line by line grants which were given to 'uneconomic but socially necessary services'. Political wisdom of the day was that only local passenger services were 'uneconomic'. Freight and long distance passenger trains had to be self supporting. So to cover the losses incurred by BR as a whole, the grant for each subsidised local passenger service had to be set at anything up to ten times the figure previously advanced in favour of closure.

LNWR 'Jumbo' 2-4-0 No. 1675 'Vimiera' at Keswick with an eastbound train of six wheel stock on 17 June 1919.   (*LCGB – Ken Nunn Collection*)

The semi derelict terminus on 1 September 1971. Driving trailer 56241 has led the two coach set in from Penrith.   (*Stuart Baker*)

Until the system was replaced in 1974, every such line had an artificially high price on its head and each year the Minister found it expedient to reject the odd grant renewal just to show that he was keeping things under control.

So in 1969, the Minister announced that the next two year grant for the Keswick line would be the last unless it survived another passage through the TUCC procedure. Then he discarded the pleas of hardship which his predecessor had upheld and ordered the line to be closed on 4 March 1972.

The remaining freight business at Flusco and Blencow lasted only until the following June.

Talk of preservation soon evaporated when it was learnt that the route would be encroached very slightly by road improvements with the cost of additional bridge work etc. falling on the preservationists and putting the whole thing out of reach.

The route from Keswick Station through the Greta Gorge to Threlkeld has been turned into 'The Railway Footpath'. This most scenic stretch can thus be enjoyed on foot. The trackbed is followed almost all the way, including the eight bowstring girder bridges which remain as a memorial to the engineer Thomas Bouch. The footpath rises to pass over the tunnel which has been filled in beneath the point where the large road viaduct goes overhead.

West of Keswick, long stretches of trackbed have been superseded by the A66 trunk road including the whole length of Bassenthwaite Lake where the eastbound carriageway occupies the railway alignment.

Designed by Thomas Bouch, architect of the ill fated Tay Bridge, the eight bowstring bridges now permit walkers to cross and recross the River Greta between Keswick and Threlkeld. Four of the bridges are upright and four inverted. One of each variety is illustrated. Located on either side of the short Wescoe Tunnel, No. 73 'Rowsome' is an inverted bowstring of 80 foot span. The steel longitudinal underneath was added in 1926 when all the bridges were strengthened to take heavier locomotives. No. 74, presumably called 'Wescoe' is of the upright variety and again the 1928 strengthening is apparent.
(Christopher George)

Post Mortem

The section west of Keswick was doomed in the 1960s because the Department of Transport had their eyes on it for road widening. But looking back after 23 years, it seems incredible that the remaining Penrith to Keswick line was able to slip away so quietly in 1972. It is, however, only since the Settle & Carlisle Campaign of the 1980s that opposition to railway closures has become a popular standpoint.

If the only problem in 1959 had been that the line was losing £50,000 per annum – and in those days nobody questioned official figures – then it is not too difficult to suggest how the matter could have been addressed.

On one side, costs could have been reduced significantly with the elimination of staff at small stations and the removal of double track and lavish signalling facilities, provided to cope with heavy mineral trains which had disappeared in the 1920s.

This was eventually done in 1967/8 but only after half the route had been closed and after political expediency had so increased published costs on the remaining section that the savings just evaporated.

The other, possibly greater, challenger would have been to increase patronage in an age when conventional wisdom dictated that growth in car ownership would soon make railways a thing of the past.

Looking at publicity for the early diesel services, one can only imagine with envy the journey opportunities and cheap fare facilities which were then on offer. Equally one suspects that these delights were only known to connoisseurs – perhaps a bit like camping coaches.

What was needed was to market the railway as a facility of use even to those who had arrived in the area by car. Success on this front was one factor which helped save the Settle & Carlisle Line. Prior to that, the idea was unheard of except for preserved lines.

Every hotel and tourist office in the Lake District will now display leaflets for the Ravenglass & Eskdale and Lakeside & Haverthwaite Railways, the Windermere steamers and probably the Settle & Carlisle line. If only . . .

Unfortunately, even as late as 1972, few of the '22,150 objectors including a dog' had yet been awakened.

With less than two weeks still to go, a Keswick bound dmu is seen at Threlkeld. The derelict signal box used to offer the incumbent a view over the station building.

(D.J. Mitchell)

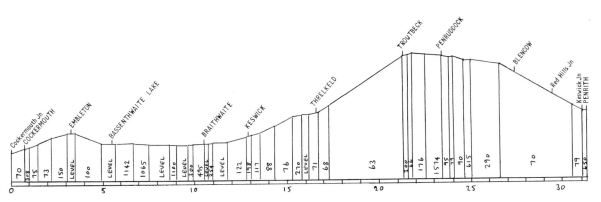

Rationalisation in evidence as a Penrith bound dmu calls at Penruddock on 21 February 1972. Costs had certainly been reduced but the accounting system had been changed so it was all in vain.   *(D.J. Mitchell)*

The 'Cauliflower' class 0-6-0s were introduced by the LNWR in the 1880s and survived for 70 years. No. 8318 is seen entering Blencow with the 9.55am Workington to Penrith on 27 August 1938.

(LCGB – Ken Nunn Collection)

46472 climbs away from the West Coast Main Line, just south of Penrith, with the 'Lakes Express'.
(David Beeken)

The 10.10am Keswick to Leeds entering Penrith on 27 August 1938. This summer Saturday working reached Leeds City at 2.05 via Ingleton.
(LCGB – Ken Nunn collection)

Environmental Protection

Opening of the Lakeside branch in 1869 marked the extent of railway development within the Lake District, at least on the standard gauge. The Ravenglass & Eskdale came in 1875, still a relatively early point in the history of railways.

Apart from the last mile of the Lakeside branch beyond Newby Bridge, the network had been built primarily with freight in mind. Local passengers were of secondary importance. Tourists were an even lower priority in an age when very few people had the time or money to travel.

There had been one or two voices raised in protest at the alleged desecration of the Lake District landscape but they were powerless against the forces lined up in support of railway building. New lines had to be approved by Parliament in which the Railway companies and owners of mineral rights were adequately represented.

Completion of the Cockermouth, Keswick & Penrith Railway opened the way for further speculation deeper into the Lake District. When a line was promoted from Windermere to Keswick in 1875, it drew opposition on a scale greater than before though it is doubtful if this would have had any effect had the scheme been founded on a stronger financial base.

In 1882, a Bill came from Parliament for the Braithwaite & Buttermere Railway. Climbing up the west of Derwentwater, this would have served the slate quarries above Honister Pass. The Bill failed mainly on financial rather than environmental grounds, but some of those who had opposed it went on to form the Lake District Defence Society.

An 1883 Bill for a 6¼ mile Ennerdale Railway, a branch off the Whitehaven, Cleator & Egremont was also unsuccessful. For the first time, the Commons Select Committee examining the Bill was instructed to consider whether the proposed line would 'injuriously affect the scenery in the neighbourhood'.

It was not just the physical intrusion of the railway which caused 'defenders' of the Lake District to take fright. It was the consequent industrial development and also the potential influx of tourists. Apparently, the natural beauty was there to be enjoyed only by those who either lived in the area or who had their own means of getting there.

1886 saw the failure of a modest proposal for a line between Windermere and Ambleside, the last occasion when a Lake District Railway Bill was presented to Parliament. A further attempt was made to reach Ambleside under the Light Railways Act 1896 first with a standard gauge line then in 1899 with a narrow gauge electric tramway. Nothing came of these proposals.

The Lake District was successfully 'defended' from further railway intrusion. The conservationists may have been helped by economic factors: the lack of freight potential and the comparatively small number of tourists in those days.

When the tourists began to arrive by road . . . well that was another story.

40099 passing through St. Bees with ICI tanks from Northwich to Corkickle on 21 July 1979. The environmental advantages of moving this traffic by rail were thrown aside when it was transferred to road during 1994
(Tom Heavyside)

The Ravenglass & Eskdale Railway

'River Irt' draws plenty of interest prior to departure from Ravenglass on 6 July 1957.   *(J.C.W. Halliday)*

'The most beautiful train journey in England'. So says publicity for this narrow gauge line which carries passengers two abreast in open or closed carriages from the coast at Ravenglass towards the peaks of the Lake District.

Uniquely amongst preserved railways, the Ravenglass & Eskdale advertises a daily service throughout the year. It saw the first application of radio signalling in the British Isles. Yet this is a line which was once so poor that it went into receivership within a year of opening to passengers. Many subsequent crises threatened its existence until, finally, it emerged as one of the Lake District's principal attractions.

The three foot gauge

The Franco Prussian War of 1870-71 prompted an upsurge in prospecting for iron ore even in the difficult territory around Eskdale. By 1873 Whitehaven Iron Mines Ltd was operating at three sites: Ban Garth, near Eskdale Green, Blea Tarn, above Beckfoot and at Nab Gill, near the village of Boot. The problem was the cost of transport to the nearest station at Drigg on the Cumbrian Coast.

A solution was sought by the promotion of a narrow gauge line running for seven miles from Boot to exchange sidings with the Furness Railway at Ravenglass.

This was authorised by the Ravenglass & Eskdale Railway Act, 1873 which rather optimistically provided for an extension down to Ravenglass harbour which was barely navigable. Share capital was subscribed half by the mine company and half by the contractor, Mr A. Oliver, who was to build the line.

Goods traffic began moving in May 1875 but the line failed to pass a Board of Trade Inspection on 29 June 1876 causing the passenger opening to be delayed until 9 November that year.

The Railway boasted two Manning Wardle 0-6-0T locos named 'Devon' after the chairman of the mine company and 'Nab Gill' after one of the mines. There were three coaches, a brake van and miscellaneous goods vehicles.

The company was in dispute with Oliver, the contractor and either could not or would not pay sums claimed by him. Oliver commenced proceedings to distrain on the company's assets but the mine company and other creditors petitioned successfully for the appointment of a receiver in the person of Henry Copland, Secretary of the Railway. He managed the Railway on behalf of the creditors until 1886 when he retired in favour of Sir Edward Moore, a partner in a London firm of chartered accountants, who remained in office until the end.

The passenger timetable varied over the 32 years of 3 foot gauge operation but there were generally five trips each way on weekdays in Summer with three on Sundays but only four trains on weekdays in Winter and no Sunday service. An extra train ran on Thursdays which was Whitehaven market day and there was an augmented service at Bank Holidays and on the day of the Fell Dales Show.

In 1880 a short branch was built to the present Dalegarth terminus near Boot in order to connect with a siding from a mine at Gill Force.

Whitehaven Iron Mines Limited went into liquidation in 1882 taking away the principal traffic for which the Railway had been built. The line struggled on for the next 26 years existing on scraps of local traffic, a bit of granite quarrying and a growing number of tourists. Bank Holiday excursions could be very busy with travellers crowding all available passenger and goods stock. By 1908, the line was very run down and it closed for the first time on 30 November that year.

A new Eskdale Railway Company was formed to lease the Railway from the receiver and the line reopened to goods traffic on 24 May 1909 coinciding with a revival of mining activity at Nab Gill. Both mining and railway operation continued intermittently until the mine was flooded on 20 December 1912. Closure followed for the second time on 30 April 1913 and that was the end of the 3 foot gauge.

The fifteen inch gauge

Narrow Gauge Railways Limited was a collaboration between R. Procter Mitchell and W.J. Bassett-Lowke operating miniature railways including those at Southport and Rhyl as well as lines on the Continent. Their activity was curtailed by the outbreak of War in 1914 leaving some of their equipment idle.

They came to Ravenglass in search of a more substantial site for a 15 inch gauge line. In July 1915 Narrow Gauge Railways Ltd took a lease over the Ravenglass & Eskdale, granted by Mr Edward Bousefield Dawson, a creditor of the old company who had no power to act.

None the less, the lessees pressed on with rebuilding and regauging. The first mile to Muncaster Mill was reopened on 28 August 1915 after which the route was progressively extended until Boot was reached in April 1917.

Initial motive power comprised two Bassett Lowke scale model engines: 4-4-2 'Sans Pareil' and 4-6-2 'Colossus'. They were not sufficiently powerful for the 1 in 38 climb beyond Beckfoot so the line was cut back to this point in the Autumn of 1918 and the terminus at Boot abandoned.

In 1922 the route was again extended but this time to the terminus at Dalegarth on the former Gill Force branch rather than to Boot itself.

The scale model engines were, as their name suggests, in the shape of main line locos at 1/4 scale. An example can be seen in the museum at

0-6-0T 'Devon' at Boot Station in three foot gauge days about 1905.   *(Martin Bairstow Collection)*

Ravenglass adjacent to the southbound BR platform. 'Synolda' which appears in the purple livery of Narrow Gauge Railways Ltd is a Bassett-Lowke product used originally on the Sand Hutton Light Railway (see *Railways in East Yorkshire*).

By contrast, the three 'Heywood' engines acquired during 1916 and 1917 were anything but scale models. They were built to the maximum which the loading gauge could accommodate regardless of aesthetic appearance. 'Ella', 'Muriel' and 'Katie' dated from 1881, 1894, and 1896 respectively. They were well worn before arrival at Ravenglass.

Sir Aubrey Brocklebank, a member of the shipping family which later controlled Cunard Line, lived at Irton Hall near Ravenglass. He began to take an interest in the narrow gauge railway from 1917. Two years later he financed the construction of an additional 'scale model' 4-6-0 which was named 'Sir Aubrey Brocklebank'.

In 1922 Sir Aubrey opened a quarry at Beckfoot using the railway to transport stone first to a crushing plant at Murthwaite and then onto the exchange sidings at Ravenglass.

The 'Heywood' engines struggled with this traffic but help came in 1923 with the delivery of 'River Esk', a 2-8-2 built specially for the line. This was based on how a main line 2-8-2 might have looked had one yet been developed. It was in 1/3 rather than 1/4 scale and is still running today.

'River Esk' was joined in 1927 by a similar machine, 0-8-2 'River Irt' which was created by reusing the frames of 'Heywood' 0-8-0 'Muriel'.

A year later, 'River Mite' appeared to complete a trio of engines named after the three rivers which converge at Ravenglass. It was created out of two of the older scale models, 'Colossus' and 'Sir Aubrey' with a little bit of 'Sans Pareil' thrown in. It was not as successful as the other two and expired in 1937.

In 1924, a dispute arose between various creditors of the old (3 foot gauge) company concerning the deal done by Dawson in 1915. Sir Aubrey Brocklebank stepped in, paid off some of the outstanding creditors and acquired the freehold for Narrow Gauge Railways Ltd over which he then assumed control in partnership with fellow ship owner, Henry Lithgow.

Six bogie hopper wagons were acquired in 1928 for the movement of granite between Murthwaite and Ravenglass. Their ability to discharge direct into standard gauge wagons greatly eased the problem of trans shipment. Their career was, however very short lived.

During 1929, a standard gauge track was laid astride the narrow gauge for 2 1/2 miles from Ravenglass to the crushing plant. Motive power was provided by a Kerr Stuart 0-6-0 diesel shunter which operated until the end of the stone traffic, and the lifting of the standard gauge in 1953. When this loco was out of action, wagons had to be chain hauled by narrow gauge locos.

The advertised passenger service of the inter war years comprised six or seven trains each weekday in Summer with just two or three on Sundays. Until 1927 there was a Winter service, except Sundays, offering just two return trips, one in the early morning and one at tea time. A Thursday only (Market Day) Winter service then continued until about 1937.

The outbreak of War caused the passenger operation to be suspended from the end of September 1939. 'River Esk' and 'River Irt' were put into store but freight traffic continued with diesel power. A limited passenger service began again in 1946. The death of Henry Lithgow in 1948 prompted the sale of both the Railway and Quarry to the Keswick Granite Company.

The new owners closed the quarrying activity in 1953 after which the Railway continued for passengers only. In September 1958 they advertised it for sale but there were no takers. The line operated normally for a further two years.

0-6-0T 'Ella' built by Heywood in 1881 and scrapped in 1926, prepares to leave Ravenglass with a bank holiday special about 1923. The old three foot gauge train shed was demolished when Ravenglass Station was rebuilt in 1928.

(Martin Bairstow Collection)

'River Irt' pauses at Irton Road en route for Ravenglass on 6 July 1957.   *(J.C.W. Halliday)*

Preservation

On 7 September 1960, it was put up for auction. By this time the Ravenglass & Eskdale Railway Preservation Society had been formed and had managed to raise about £5,000. This was not enough but the Society was supported by Mr Colin Gilbert, a Midlands stockbroker.

There were scrap merchants in the hall as the Railway was offered first as a going concern. The Society bid £10,000, someone else ventured £11,000 and the Society came back with £12,000. The auctioneer invited further bids rising in hundreds but there was silence. The alternative of selling the assets piecemeal never arose.

Mr Gilbert assumed control but he died in 1968 when his interest was acquired by Sir Wavell Wakefield MP. The Society loaned its £5,000 to the new Ravenglass & Eskdale Railway Company Ltd and adopted a supporting role with volunteer members supplementing the work of the full time staff.

For a brief period between 1964 and 1966, there was a revival of freight traffic with granite blocks being moved from Murthwaite to Irton Road but the enterprise folded.

On the passenger side, the Railway has expanded. During the 1960s, there were generally six advertised trips each way in Summer but with the facility to run extras. Sometimes two trains might run in one timetable path thanks to permissive block working. The loop at Irton Road was long enough to pass two trains in each direction.

Line capacity was improved in 1975 with additional loops at Miteside and Fisherground dividing the route into four sections of roughly equal length.

Radio Control

An accident occurred in 1976 when 'River Esk' collided head on with 'Shelagh of Eskdale'. This quickly led to the introduction of radio signalling, the first such application in the British Isles. As described in *Modern Railways* (November 1978), the system is basically a form of central traffic control by which the signalman at Ravenglass can control movements through all four absolute block sections. Before a train leaves Ravenglass, the driver is issued with a sheet showing his outward and return paths. He is given verbal instruction to proceed through the first section to Miteside and he marks this in his sheet with an arrow. Approaching Miteside, he speaks to the signalman by radio. He may be given instruction to go on to Irton Road, which he will mark on his sheet, or he may be told to enter the passing loop and wait. All movements and messages are recorded by the signalman.

Maximum line capacity is now a train every 20 minutes in each direction. The advertised service varies with the time of year rising to 15 trains each way on peak days in mid Summer. The line operates throughout the year, a limited Winter service having been reintroduced soon after the new régime took over in 1960.

On Monday to Fridays throughout the year, there is an early departure from Eskdale at 7.25am for which purpose a diesel is stabled there overnight. This is primarily a staff train but is advertised to the public. From November to March it is the only working of the day, returning from Ravenglass at 4.10pm. From April until October there is a basic hourly daytime service which is supplemented on busy days. On Winter Saturdays and Sundays, there are two return trips in the afternoon. The Ravenglass & Eskdale offers the most comprehensive passenger timetable of any preserved railway which is no small achievement

given the sparsely populated area through which it runs.

In 1960, motive power comprised only 'River Esk', 'River Irt' and an 0-4-4 steam outline diesel. Dating from 1933, this was never considered worthy of a name nor a number.

Since then, four new locomotives have been built: two steam and two diesel. 'River Mite', delivered in 1966 is a 2-8-2 similar to 'River Esk'. 'Northern Rock' is a 2-6-2 rather more 'narrow gauge' than 'miniature' in appearance. It was built at Ravenglass and completed in 1976.

'Shelagh of Eskdale' is a 4-6-4 diesel hydraulic which entered service in 1969. It is loosely modelled on a main line loco with a cab at either end. 'Lady Wakefield' is a 0-4-4-0 diesel mechanical with only one cab.

Rolling stock comprises a mixture of open and closed carriages. Train formations can be varied to suit the weather.

The steam outline diesel loco, rebuilt in 1933 out of an earlier petrol tractor, stands under the bridge at Irton Road on 4 October 1958.

(J.C.W. Halliday)

'Royal Anchor', a scale model diesel hydraulic purchased by the RER in 1961, has just arrived at Dalegarth on Friday 3 March 1972 with the afternoon train from Ravenglass, a single coach which in winter is used primarily by the Railway's own staff.

(D.J. Mitchell)

4-6-2 'Sir Aubrey Brocklebank'
at Ravenglass on 20 June
1920.
(LCGB - Ken Nunn collection)

2-8-2 'River Mite' then in only
its second year of operation,
entering Ravenglass Station in
September 1968. The signal
box was then under
construction.

(John F Oxley)

Originally a 2ft gauge 0-4-0
well tank from Dundee Gas
Works, 'Bonnie Dundee' was
converted into a 0-4-2T. It is
seen on 24 October 1983
having just turned on the
turntable at Eskdale to face
back to Ravenglass. Scafell
forms the back cloth.

(David Beeken)

'Northern Rock' replenishes its water supply on 11 September 1993. Eskdale bound steam trains usually pause at this water column which is located just beyond Fisherground crossing loop. *(Martin Bairstow)*

2-6-2 'Northern Rock' leaving The Green for Eskdale (Dalegarth) on 15 July 1978. *(Tom Heavyside)*

Getting There

'Getting to the Lakes couldn't be easier with Inter City's fast air conditioned coaches and catering facilities' – so claims a glossy BR leaflet entitled 'The Lakes & Beyond'. In 1994 this offered a range of discounts on hotel accommodation, restaurants and tourist attractions to holders of rail tickets (including rovers) valid to any station between Lancaster and Carlisle including the Morecambe and Windermere branches, the Furness and Cumbrian Coast Lines.

Unfortunately, the rail network scarcely penetrates the Lake District, a drawback which this leaflet fails to recognise. Certainly you can get a discount at the Laurel & Hardy Museum in Ulverston, at Tullie House in Carlisle or at the Judges' lodgings in Lancaster, but if you want to visit Coniston, Ullswater or Derwentwater, then these do not, apparently, come within the orbit of 'The Lakes & Beyond'.

There is reference to the availability of through tickets to Ambleside and Grasmere but this is the extent of any meaningful information on connecting bus services. The free pocket timetable for Manchester - Barrow/Windermere gives bus times to Ambleside but not Grasmere. The national railway timetable is totally silent.

In fact it would be quite easy to reach Keswick, the most important place without a direct rail service, as buses depart from outside the stations at both Windermere and Penrith. There has, at some time since the rail closure, been a through ticket to Keswick via Penrith but it went the way of most 'one off' facilities which hardly anybody knows about.

My 1934 LMS timetable shows bus times to Ullswater, from both Windermere and Penrith, also between Windermere and Keswick and in connection with the Windermere and Coniston steamers. This information would therefore have been available at any LMS station or travel agent throughout the United Kingdom which is certainly not the case today.

Closure of just 18 miles of track has, in practice, thrown away almost all rail traffic bound for Keswick even though it remains perfectly feasible to travel by train as far as Penrith. There you may change on to a bus with scarcely any more effort than was previously required to board the branch dmu. Simplicity itself if only the information were readily available.

In August 1972, Stuart Baker and I had a seven day North West Rover ticket. We travelled over 1,600 miles by train and steamer on a carefully planned itinerary. We needed a bus on the final day to get eight miles from Newby Bridge to Ulverston, somebody having closed the Lakeside branch seven years previously. In the course of the week, we enquired without success at various bus stations between Southport and Carlisle, finally tracking down a timetable at Carlisle Railway Station.

In September 1990, Philippa and I decided to support the efforts of Cumbria County Council to

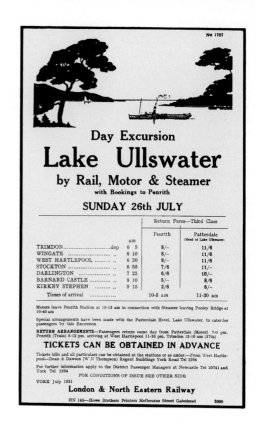

promote bus links off the Settle & Carlisle Line. Alighting from the train at Langwathby, we searched in vain for so much as a sign marked 'bus stop'. Would the Keswick bus drive up to the station or should we walk down to the main road? – no indication there either. Our sole fellow traveller was more lost than we were, a visitor from the USA who declared a belief in 'public transportation'.

20 minutes after the advertised time, we were on the point of giving up but then we flagged down a bus which was, in fact, on a through journey from Newcastle to Keswick. It took the driver a little time to work out the fare but then we were off. The system had worked. The journey from Langwathby to Keswick only takes 45 minutes creating enormous opportunities if only they were co-ordinated effectively.

What is needed is a strategic network of buses, achieved largely by harnessing services which are running already. Times must be fixed for the duration of the railway timetable in which they should appear as a fully integrated part of the system with through ticketing. In other words it should be as easy to book to Cockermouth or Coniston as it is to Barrow or Burneside.

The buses would continue to carry their own indigenous traffic in addition. If anyone doubts that this idea is feasible, then they need only wait until we publish *Railways Around Lake Luzern*.

Conclusion

I am grateful as always to John Halliday for help with photographs, in particular for his having taken the trouble in 1957 and 1958 to record two branch lines which he feared were going to close.

The owners of both the Ravenglass & Eskdale Railway and the Coniston branch had evidently decided that they had no further interest in them.

The Keswick Granite Company offered the Eskdale line for sale, keeping it running to allow time for a preservation society to raise funds. Then they sold the line at scrap value as a going concern. John was able to take out life membership of the society to help ensure its survival.

Somewhat in contrast, British Railways simply closed the Coniston branch, demolished it and sold the right of way piecemeal. Sale to an alternative operator did not come within the 'careful consideration' which BR supposedly undertook before embarking on this course.

It is certainly ironic, that the Ravenglass & Eskdale Railway, which went into receivership as long ago as 1877 and which first closed as early as 1908, should now be enjoying a period of prosperity when other, more important Lake District lines have disappeared.

At the inauguration of 'River Mite' on 20 May 1967, the Chairman of Cumberland County Council declared that his Council was 'entirely in favour of the continuance of such a line as the R & E R' adding that 'we are absolutely determined that we are not going to turn the Lake District into a gigantic car park'.

So when, shortly afterwards, the Lakeside Railway Society looked serious in its bid to preserve the entire branch from Plumpton Junction, the neighbouring Lancashire County Council exercised its powers to purchase two short bits of the line for the purpose of road widening. It would have increased the cost of the road scheme only marginally to have preserved the integrity of the railway. There is still room for a single track between the road and the estuary at Greenodd but a bridge would have been needed just south of Haverthwaite.

The result is that instead of providing a means of access to the Lake District, the truncated preserved line merely offers a short excursion for people who have already reached there by car.

An even greater loss was that of the only route through northern Lakeland. Closure west of Keswick took place when the Beeching axe was in full swing. It was a serious setback but one which ought to have been tempered by the reprieve of the more important section between Penrith and Keswick. Had this survived just another year or so, beyond

Most definitely not John Halliday's last trip on the Ravenglass & Eskdale Railway but by the late 1950s the outlook was beginning to look rather bleak. Things have improved since.   (J.C.W. Halliday)

1972, then it is highly probable that it would still be open today doing business similar to the Windermere branch.

The Keswick line fell foul of an arbitrary accounting formula which held sway between 1968 and 1974 and which was responsible for a number of quite serous closures in that period. After 1974, the size of the BR network tended to stabilise and then to expand slightly.

So the Lake District has become a gigantic car park. Those whose ancestors sought to protect the area's natural beauty by heading off railway expansion have failed miserably in stemming an infinitely greater intrusion by motor transport.

We are now moving slowly towards a consensus that we cannot allow the unlimited growth of motor traffic in our towns and cities. Who would ever have believed in the 1960s that we would now be witnessing the return of electric trams in Manchester and Sheffield?

Car ownership is expected to double again within the next generation. Surely the extra journeys are not all going to be in city centres. People are going to travel to work less not more often. It is the tourist areas which are going to bear the brunt of the extra congestion.

I seem to recall Transport Minister John Peyton predicting that 'one day we may have to reinvent the tram'. It was about the time that he approved the

Penrith to Keswick closure. Perhaps one day we may also have to reinvent the rural railway – at least in selected areas. It shouldn't be too difficult. Most of the formation is still there between Penrith and Keswick as it is between Plumpton Junction and Haverthwaite.

In the meantime at least a second best option could be had simply by integrating strategic bus links as feeders to the rail network.

A predictable new use for that once proud Coniston terminus.

(Martin Bairstow)

143609 on the 10.00 ex Windermere does worthwhile business at Oxenholme on 21 July 1990, a scene which ought to be repeated at Penrith and Ulverston with passengers changing between the branch and the main line – but it isn't.

(Tom Heavyside)

Appendices

Carnforth and Barrow

Opened

3. 6.1846	Barrow – Crooklands (goods)
12. 8.1846	Barrow – Dalton (passenger)
6. 5.1851	Crooklands – Lindal
7. 6.1854	Lindal – Ulverston
26. 8.1857	Ulverston – Carnforth

Miles	Stations	Opened	Closed
0	Carnforth	22. 9.1846	—
3¾	Silverdale	26. 8.1857	—
6	Arnside	1858	—
9¼	Grange Over Sands	26. 8.1857	—
11½	Kents Bank	26. 8.1857	—
13½	Cark & Cartmel	26. 8.1857	—
19½	Ulverston	7. 6.1854	—
21	Lindal	6. 5.1851	31. 7.1951
22¾	Dalton	12. 8.1846	—
24¼	Furness Abbey	1847	25. 9.1950
27	Roose	1850	—
—	Barrow Town	12. 8.1846	31. 5.1881
28¾	Barrow Central	1. 6.1882	—
—	Ramsden Dock	1. 6.1881	May 1915
—	Island Road	1. 5.1899	31.12.1966

Barrow, Whitehaven and Workington

Opened

18. 5.1846	Harrington – Workington
3. 6.1846	Barrow – Kirkby (goods)
	(via Furness Abbey)
12. 8.1846	Barrow – Harrington (passenger)
15. 2.1847	Whitehaven – Harrington (goods)
19. 3.1847	Whitehaven – Harrington (passenger)
Feb. 1848	Kirkby – Broughton
21. 7.1849	Ravenglass – Whitehaven Newtown
8. 7.1850	Bootle – Ravenglass
1.11.1850	Broughton – Bootle
30. 9.1852	Whitehaven Tunnel
3.12.1855	(Newtown closed to passengers)
1. 8.1858	Dalton and Foxfield Curves
1. 6.1882	Barrow Central – Park South Jn.

Miles	Stations	Opened	Closed
0	Barrow Central	1. 6.1882	—
6	Askam	1. 4.1868	—
9¼	Kirkby in Furness	3. 6.1846	—
11¼	Foxfield	1. 8.1858	—
13½	Green Road	1853	—
16	Millom	1.11.1850	—
19	Silecroft	1.11.1850	—
24½	Bootle	8. 7.1850	—
20	Eskmeals	8. 7.1850	1. 8.1959
29¼	Ravenglass	21. 7.1849	—
31	Drigg	21. 7.1849	—
33¼	Seascale	21. 7.1849	—
35	Sellafield	21. 7.1849	—
37	Braystones	21. 7.1849	—
38¼	Nethertown	21. 7.1849	—
41¼	St. Bees	21. 7.1849	—
—	Whitehaven Newtown	21. 7.1849	3.12.1855
44¾	Corkickle	3.12.1855	—
45¾	Whitehaven Bransty	19. 3.1847	—
47	Parton	19. 3.1847	—
50½	Harrington	18. 5.1846	—
52¼	Workington Main	19. 1.1846	—

Ulverston and Lakeside

Opened

1. 6.1869	opened throughout
5. 9.1965	Closed to passengers and to all
	traffic Haverthwaite – Lakeside
21. 4.1967	closed Plumpton Jn. – Haverthwaite
2. 5.1973	reopened Haverthwaite – Lakeside

Miles	Stations	Opened	Closed
0	Ulverston	26. 8.1857	—
3¾	Greenodd	1. 6.1869	30. 9.1946
6½	Haverthwaite	1. 6.1869	30. 9.1946
8	Newby Bridge	1905	12. 9.1939
9½	Lakeside	1. 6.1869	5. 9.1965

Workington, Keswick and Penrith

Opened

28. 4.1847	Workington – Cockermouth
26.10.1864	Cockermouth – Penrith (goods)
2. 1.1865	Cockermouth – Penrith (passenger)
5. 9.1866	Redhills Jn. – Eamont Jn. (goods)

Closed

June 1938	Redhills Jn. – Eamont Jn.
16. 4.1966	Workington – Keswick
4. 3.1972	Keswick – Penrith

The line between Flusco Quarry
and Penrith remained open for goods
until 16 June 1972

Miles	Stations	Opened	Closed
0	Workington Main	19. 1.1846	—
1¼	Workington Bridge	28. 4.1847	30.12.1951
3¼	Camerton	29. 4.1847	1. 3.1952
4½	Marron Junction	2. 4.1866	30. 6.1897
5¾	Broughton Cross	28. 4.1847	28. 2.1942
6½	Brigham	28. 4.1847	16. 4.1966
9	Cockermouth	28. 4.1847	16. 4.1966
11¾	Embleton	2. 1.1865	13. 9.1958
14¼	Bassenthwaite Lake	2. 1.1865	16. 4.1966
19¼	Braithwaite	2. 1.1865	16. 4.1966
21½	Keswick	2. 1.1865	4. 3.1972
22½	Briery Bobbin	1922	15.11.1958
25	Threlkeld	2. 1.1865	4. 3.1972
27¾	Highgate	17. 8.1908	Dec. 1928
29¾	Troutbeck	2. 1.1865	4. 3.1972
32	Penruddock	2. 1.1865	4. 3.1972
36	Blencow	2. 1.1865	4. 3.1972
39¾	Penrith	17.12.1846	—

Oxenholme, Kendal and Windermere

Opened

22. 9.1846	Oxenholme – Kendal
21. 4.1847	Kendal – Windermere

Miles	Stations	Opened	Closed
0	Oxenholme	22. 9.1846	—
2	Kendal	22. 9.1846	—
4	Burneside	21. 4.1847	—
6½	Staveley	21. 4.1847	—
10¼	Windermere	21. 4.1847	—

Arnside and Hincaster Junction

26. 6.1876	Opened
4. 5.1942	Closed to passengers
7. 9.1963	Closed Sandside – Hincaster Jun.
Jan. 1972	Closed Arnside – Sandside

Miles	Stations	Opened	Closed
0	Arnside	1858	—
2	Sandside	26. 6.1876	4. 5.1942
3½	Heversham	1. 7.1890	4. 5.1942
5	Hincaster Junction	—	—

Ravenglass & Eskdale

Date	Event	Miles	Station	Opened	Closed
May 1875	Opened to goods	0	Ravenglass (R & E)	9.11.1876	—
9.11.1876	Opened to passengers	1¼	Muncaster Mill	9.11.1876	—
30.11.1908	Closed to passengers	4¼	Irton Road	9.11.1876	—
30. 4.1913	Closed to all traffic	4¾	The Green	9.11.1876	—
28. 8.1915	Reopened and regauged	6½	Beckfoot	9.11.1876	—
to Apr 1917		7	Eskdale (Dalegarth)	1922	—
		7¼	Boot	9.11.1876	Aug. 1918

Foxfield & Coniston

Date	Event	Miles	Station	Opened	Closed
Opened					
Feb. 1848	Foxfield – Broughton	0	Foxfield	1. 8.1858	—
18. 6.1859	Broughton – Coniston	1¼	Broughton	Feb. 1848	4.10.1958
		3¾	Woodland	18. 6.1859	4.10.1958
4.10.1958	Closed to passengers	7½	Torver	18. 6.1859	4.10.1958
28. 4.1962	Closed to goods	9¾	Coniston	18. 6.1859	4.10.1958

Ulverston and Conishead Priory

Date	Event	Miles	Station	Opened	Closed
27. 6.1883	Opened	0	Ulverston	26. 8.1857	—
31.12.1916	Closed to passengers and to all traffic	2¼	North Lonsdale	June 1888	31.12.1916
	North Lonsdale to Conishead Priory	3½	Conishead Priory	27. 6.1883	31.12.1916

Barrow and Piel

Date	Event	Miles	Station	Opened	Closed
3. 6.1846	Opened to goods	0	Barrow Central	1. 6.1882	—
12. 8.1846	Opened to passengers	1¼	Salthouse	22. 5.1920	6. 7.1936
1873	Salthouse Curve	3¼	Rampside	1846	6. 7.1936
6. 7.1936	Closed	4	Piel	1846	6. 7.1936

Whitehaven, Cleator and Egremont

Date	Event	Miles	Station	Opened	Closed
	Opened to goods	0	Whitehaven Bransty	19. 3.1847	—
1.11.1856	Corkickle – Egremont	1	Corkickle	30. 9.1852	—
1.11.1856	Moor Row – Frizington	4	Moor Row	1. 6.1857	7. 1.1935
Nov. 1862	Frizington – Lamplugh	5¼	Woodend	1. 3.1880	7. 1.1935
15. 1.1866	Lamplugh – Marron Junction	6½	Egremont	1. 6.1857	7. 1.1935
2. 8.1869	Egremont – Sellafield	9½	Beckermet	2. 8.1869	7. 1.1935
	Opened to passengers	11½	Sellafield	21. 7.1849	—
1. 7.1857	Corkickle – Egremont	5	Cleator Moor	1. 6.1857	13. 4.1931
1. 7.1857	Moor Row – Frizington	6¼	Frizington	1. 6.1857	13. 4.1931
1. 2.1864	Frizington – Rowrah	7¾	Yeathouse	1. 2.1864	13. 4.1931
2. 4.1866	Rowrah – Marron Junction	8½	Winder	1. 2.1864	13. 4.1931
2. 8.1869	Egremont – Sellafield	9½	Rowrah	1. 2.1864	13. 4.1931
	Closed to passengers	11½	Lamplugh	2. 4.1866	13. 4.1931
13. 4.1931	Moor Row – Marron Junction	13	Ullock	2. 4.1866	13. 4.1931
7. 1.1935	Corkickle – Sellafield	14¼	Branthwaite	2. 4.1866	13. 4.1931
	Closed to all traffic	17¼	Bridgefoot	2. 4.1866	13. 4.1931
3. 5.1954	Rowrah – Marron Junction	18	Marron Junction	2. 4.1866	30. 6.1897
18. 1.1970	Beckermet – Sellafield				
1978	Moor Row – Rowrah				
3.10.1980	Corkickle – Beckermet				

A workmen's service operated between Moor Row and Sellafield until 4 September 1965.

A 'Derby Lightweight' set leaving Blencow for Keswick on 30 August 1964. The signalman wanders back to his box with the token which he has collected from the driver.
(Douglas Butterfield)